Raise
Confident and *Responsible*
Kids

111 Common-Sense Tips

by
Dee Dees

LifeGuides Press
Gilbert, Arizona

Raise Confident and Responsible Kids:
111 Common-Sense Tips
Dee Dees

First published in 2012
LifeGuides Press
Gilbert, AZ 85295
(480) 703-1244

Website: www.raiseconfidentkids.com

ISBN: 978-0-9667829-2-9
Printed and bound in the United States of America

DEDICATION

This book is dedicated to my husband Fred,
who has been an amazing father,
and a wonderful partner in my life…

and to our two adult children,
Joel and Jennifer,
who have become more than I could have wished for.
They are confident, responsible, fascinating adults
whom I'm proud to call my kids
as well as my best friends.

Raise Confident and Responsible Kids
111 Common-Sense Ideas
Dee Dees

Table of Contents

Introduction

Love	1
Communication	13
Example	29
Discipline	37
Encouragement	55
People Building	63
Respect	71
Responsibility	79
Self Esteem	89
Time	103
Values	115

INTRODUCTION

Parenting is a tough job. While there are thousands of books on the topic, there is no "instruction manual" as such. We learn by doing. Often, we learn by doing what our parents did—which wasn't always the best route to go.

My husband and I both came from loving—though not demonstrative—families. But our parents were not particularly supportive of our goals or dreams, and there wasn't a college graduate among them. There was never any expectation that either of us would go to college.

Fred and I took all the attributes we felt we'd missed out on; encouragement, respect, physical affection, high—but not unreasonable—expectations, support, and more, and lavished these on our children. "I love you" was heard in our home more often than "where's the clicker?" They always knew they were loved, even when discipline was necessary.

We were not perfect parents by any means, but our kids became well-behaved, confident teenagers, and then responsible, caring adults. I was asked once what we "did right" to raise two kids that anyone would be proud of. I had to think about it, because I didn't believe we had done anything special. And we'd made our share of mistakes.

I finally realized, it wasn't any big thing we had done, it was all the little things, that just seemed to be common sense to me. But then I'd hear a mother screaming at her kids in the grocery story, or see a dad telling his child three times to do something, being ignored, and not taking action. And it occurred to me that common-sense parenting wasn't as prevalent as I had assumed.

When I asked my daughter what she felt we had done "right" in parenting, her answer was *"You always showed us love when we were little, and always supported us in whatever we did."*

Obviously there is more to parenting than love and support, but those two traits go a long way toward building confident and responsible kids. My hope is that the common-sense ideas in this book will help inspire parents to be more patient and loving, and in turn, create more confident, responsible, and caring children.

A few disclaimers
For parents of troubled children:

This book is not intended to solve major behavioral problems - I leave that for the psychologists, counselors or medical doctors. Its purpose is simply to provide some ideas for becoming better parents, raising children with healthy self-esteem and confidence, and teaching children—through example—to become responsible, caring adults.

For unique family situations:

Throughout the book, I refer to a Mom and/or Dad as the parents raising their children. While I recognize that there are many other types of family and caregiver situations (same-sex partners, grandparents, foster parents, and so on) I refer to Mom and Dad for the sake of simplicity. The point is not *who* is raising the kids, it's *how* they are raising them.

For the grammarphiles:

Most examples in this book refer to a specific gender, alternating between male and female. But in some cases, examples use a singular noun, (your child, a kid) followed later by a plural "they." The author understands that—technically—this is incorrect, (though it's becoming more accepted) but constantly writing "he or she" or "his/her" becomes awkward to read. The author hopes you will look past the technical aspect and focus on the content.

~~~~~~~~~~~~~~~~~~~~~~~~~~~~~~~)(~~~~~~~~~~~~~~~~~~~~~~~

LOVE

"...but the greatest of these is Love."

A happy, fulfilled life begins with love. Most prison inmates will tell you that as youngsters, they were abused, neglected, or felt unloved. That's not an excuse, but it is a catalyst for sending children off on the wrong track of life. Love can overcome so much. That's why it's the first chapter in this book. The Bible describes love better than I ever could, in First Corinthians.

"Love is patient, love is kind. It does not envy, it does not boast, it is not proud. It is not rude, it is not self-seeking, it is not easily angered, it keeps no record of wrongs. Love does not delight in evil but rejoices with the truth. It always protects, always trusts, always hopes, always perseveres.

"And now these three remain: faith, hope and love. But the greatest of these is love."

1 Corinthians 13 Verses 4-7 & 13

~~~~~~~~~~~~~~~~~~~~~~~~~~~~~)(~~~~~~~~~~~~~~~~~~~~~~~

Tell them you love them!

It's just that easy. When they leave the house, when you hang up the phone with them, when they go to bed, when you end a conversation, whenever you darn well feel like it … just say "*I love you.*"

Neither my husband nor I heard those words very often growing up, but when our kids came along, we were determined that there would be no doubt in their minds that they were loved.

Even if those words haven't always come easily in your family, begin to use them now. You will be surprised at what a difference it can make.

There are children who grow to adulthood without ever being told they are loved. Don't let your child be one of those. Even if they don't respond, every time they leave the house they will know without a doubt how you feel about them. There's no greater gift you can give your children than that knowledge.

...and it could make all the difference in the world!

How I've accomplished this:

Show them you love them!

Sending your children off into the world with a hug, kiss or pat on the back, is a perfect way to let them know you love them. It not only reinforces your love and commitment, but gives them a sense of security, that they are part of a solid home. It lets them know that you enjoy being with them, and that they are important to you. Younger kids usually love being hugged and kissed, or patted on the head or the back.

However, once they reach the teen years, some may shy away from too much touchy-feely emotion. If they do, respect their wishes, and don't embarrass them by planting a big kiss on their cheek in public or in front of friends. Just try to sneak in the occasional hug when you can. If they complain too much, tell them you know *they* don't need it—but *you* do! They'll probably understand and respect your need, and will secretly appreciate that you still want to feel that closeness with them.

Make this a commitment that you won't break: even if you've just finished disciplining your child; even if the two of you are at odds over a chore or a broken rule; even if you're in a bad mood. *Always* give a hug, and say "I love you," before you or they leave the house.

A hug is the shortest distance between a parent and child.

How I've accomplished this:

Smile and Laugh often!

A smile can work wonders—especially if either you or your child is tired, frustrated, or has other negative emotions going on.

If you're the one having a bad day, you don't have to completely bury your emotions, but an easy smile can let your little one know that it's not *her* you're upset with. That simple act can alleviate her fears and help calm her, and should make you feel better as well.

It has been proven that laughter can relieve stress, make us happier, and even make us healthier. You can set the standard by laughing and smiling often.

If, on the other hand, your child is the one down in the dumps, smiling can let her know you understand, and maybe even communicate that things are not as bad as they seem. A smile or laugh from you is reassuring that all is well with her world.

A smile is the shortest distance between any *two people.*

How I've accomplished this:

Love Unconditionally

It's great to praise and compliment your child often. But if too many of the compliments are attached to what he has done, he may begin to feel that if he stops achieving or behaving well, your love may also stop. He may fear he has to strive for perfection in order to earn your love.

It's fine to say, for instance, *"Great job with the report card! I'm so proud that you got all 'A's,"* then add, *"But I love you for yourself, and I'm happy that you're my son."*

Also be sure to express your love when they try something and fail. *"Don't feel bad about fumbling the ball; I know you did your best, and I'm still proud of you and love you."* Children need love and acceptance more than they need praise for accomplishments.

Don't tie your love to their behavior, good or bad. Even when they misbehave, break a rule, or throw a tantrum, it's important that they know you still love them, but will not tolerate their behavior.

Pride in their actions is good. Love for who they are is better!

How I've accomplished this:

Tuck them in when they're little

There's nothing better than a good old tuck-in for showing love and providing security for little ones. It's that last reassurance at night that you will still be there in the morning. It's the shooing out of monsters, a saying of prayers, a final opportunity to have a few moments of quality quiet time, with just the two of you. Even if you're rushed, tired, or still have mountains of laundry, try to spend at least five or ten minutes with each child at bedtime, talking and reinforcing your love for them.

Even when my daughter was in her early teens, I'd go in and talk a few minutes after she was in bed. Often some of her concerns about fitting in, or some other teen-related issue would surface, though they hadn't come up in earlier conversations. There was something about the darkness and sanctuary of her room that allowed her to share her feelings more easily.

Those last few minutes talking with you might alleviate the worries of the day. It will be time well spent.

Make their last moments before falling asleep pleasant ones!

How I've accomplished this:

Plan little surprises

Who doesn't love a surprise? And kids are more receptive than anyone when it comes to an unexpected treat. Put a favorite (but unanticipated) snack in their lunch boxes. Leave them little notes. Get them a CD or book they've been talking about. Pick them up from school and take them someplace fun. Plan a trip to an amusement park when they least expect it.

We occasionally picked up our kids from school at lunchtime and took them somewhere for a quick bite. Their small school was amenable to this, and the kids always enjoyed the unexpected trip!

Plan mother-daughter, father-son or vice-versa outings. Surprises tell a child that life is more than work, school, bills and routine. It tells them that you're thinking about them and that you want to bring a bit of unexpected pleasure into their lives.

Life is full of surprises...make sure you provide the good ones!

How I've accomplished this:

Pay attention to their interests

When you take notice of what Joey listens to, reads, watches, or enjoys, you demonstrate that you care about his interests. If you pay attention to his choices in music, books and movies, you can have discussions with him about what he likes and why. You may enjoy bopping to the oldies, but your teen may prefer groups whose names you can't even pronounce. With some of the violent song lyrics that are popular now, it's important that we know what our kids are listening to.

Bite the bullet and listen to some of his music. If you don't approve of it, you'll be able to discuss it with him. Ask him what it is about those lyrics that appeals to him. Tell him why you don't approve, offer options, and make some decisions that will suit everyone concerned.

Be able to discuss other interests as well. If Justin is developing a love for baseball, and closely follows the home team, you might want to read up on the sport, the players, and the stats yourself. Think how impressed he'll be when you can discuss the pitcher's style or get excited with him when his favorite player breaks the home-run record.

Just don't get so involved that you end up taking over, and pushing him out of his own area of interest. Learn enough so you can discuss it with him, but don't start showing off that you know more than he does.

Showing interest in what others do is more encouraging than praise.

How I've accomplished this:

Greet them enthusiastically

Imagine a child arriving home from school excited and looking forward to sharing her news with Mom, only to hear her mother yell *"Don't walk on the kitchen floor, I just mopped it."* It kind of takes all the oomph out of her excitement.

Think how much better you'll both feel if you're ready for your children's arrival, and can give them a big hug and spend time hearing about their day. My daughter, now married with children of her own, still talks about how much she looked forward to coming home from school and seeing me.

If your job means that they arrive home before you do, be sure you seek them out as soon as you get home, and let them know you've been looking forward all day to seeing them. Take a few minutes to catch up on their activities, and give them your undivided attention before starting household chores.

Showing your joy at seeing them is loving and reassuring.

How I've accomplished this:

Provide a feeling of security

A part of feeling loved is feeling secure about our environment. In the aftermath of tragedies such as September 11th or Hurricane Katrina, feeling secure is a little more difficult; especially when children don't quite comprehend what they hear. Help them understand that no matter what happens, you will always love and care for them, and that they will always have a stable home.

We all realize that many things happen which are out of our control; but reassuring our kids that they'll always be taken care of will bring some relief.

If you're going through a divorce, assure the kids that both parents will always love them even though they live apart. If they worry about losing one of you, explain that although there are no guarantees, the likelihood is small, and that you will do all you can to keep everyone from harm.

If they're concerned about what would become of them if they lost both parents, make arrangements that they will feel comfortable with (grandparents, aunt and uncle, etc.,) and explain those arrangements to the children. Then reassure them that it's extremely unlikely that anything will happen.

However, *don't* make statements such as *"I promise I'll never die and leave you."* If they're old enough, they'll know you have no control over that, and they won't trust other promises you make.

Never underestimate the security that personal contact provides.

How I've accomplished this:

Send them out happy

One of my most devastating parenting memories is that of screaming at my kids for something they did or didn't do before going to school one morning. They were crying, I was screaming, and then … the carpool mom was honking the horn to pick them up. As they rushed out the door, still in tears, I broke down, realizing I was sending them off to school in emotional turmoil. I called the school and asked that they bring the kids to the office to call home as soon as they could. I emphasized that it was important, but not an emergency. I needed the *kids* to know I loved them and I was sorry for my behavior. And *I* needed to know they wouldn't have that last angry scene hanging over them the rest of the day.

A child going to school upset, angry or in tears, will likely dwell on the negative beginning to his or her day, making it more difficult to concentrate and learn.

Strive always to keep a calm, positive environment for your kids, but especially before sending them out of the house for any length of time. You want them to have good feelings about—and look forward to—coming home, and the family they're returning to.

As the morning goes, so goes the day. Give them a great start!

How I've accomplished this:

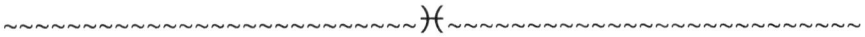

COMMUNICATION

*"The single biggest problem in communication
is the illusion that it has taken place."*
~ George Bernard Shaw

Communication generally refers to one person speaking while others listen; or writing something that others will read. There's so much more to it than that; namely that the most important part of communication is not the speaking, or even the listening, but the *understanding* of what was meant to be communicated. That's where most of us miss the boat at one time or another.

In communicating with our children, we need to express ourselves clearly, leaving no room for misunderstanding. It's our job as parents to make sure our children understand exactly what we say, what we mean, and what we expect from them.

But communication is not just about relating rules and expectations, it should also be about expressing love, respect, gratitude, interest, care and concern. Nothing happens between any two people without communication. It's critical that we learn how to do it right.

~~~~~~~~~~~~~~~~~~~~~~~~~~~~)(~~~~~~~~~~~~~~~~~~~~~~~~~

Ask about their day

Most of us like to tell others about our experiences; to share in the joy of good ones, and even complain about the not-so-good. But sometimes a child is reluctant to open up with adults—even parents—especially if we seem busy or inattentive.

If we make it a point to ask how his or her day went, and pay close attention to the response, we demonstrate that they're important to us and that we're interested in what happens in their lives.

If their responses are brief or non-committal, ask more open-ended questions, or ones that will draw more details from them. Be careful not to seem as though you're prying into an issue they may not be ready to talk about, but if you let them know you're truly interested, they'll be more likely to open up and share with you.

> *Listen to the little things today,*
> *and they'll share the bigger ones tomorrow!*

How I've accomplished this:

Talk about your day

Let your children know how your day was. If you had a great day, be sure to share that with your children. Tell them the good things that happened; perhaps someone performed an act of kindness for you or paid you a compliment; or maybe you helped a stranger, and felt good about it. Help your children see that attitude can sometimes make the difference between a so-so day and a great one.

If you had to face some particular challenges, tell your children about those and how you handled them (keep the explanation simple enough for your child's age level) but don't get into a habit of complaining about every perceived wrong, the jerk who cut you off in traffic, or the slowpoke in the checkout line. If you had a bad day, explain that some things didn't go as well as you had hoped, and you're a little discouraged about it. Then make it clear that your family is not responsible—and be sure you don't take out your frustrations on them.

Good day or bad day; demonstrate that you're still the same parent.

How I've accomplished this:

Recognize their moods

Sometimes children will hem and haw and ask seemingly off-the-wall questions. That's usually a good sign that there's something on their minds they need to discuss with you. If you are receptive to their comments, take them seriously, and don't brush them off as being trivial or silly, children will be more likely to open up.

On the other hand, sometimes no matter how much you try, they just don't want to talk. Unless it's a regular occurrence, recognize that they may just be having an off day, may have had a spat with a friend, or just "don't want to talk about it." We, as adults, occasionally have times like that. We need to allow our children the same feelings, as long as it's not an on-going circumstance.

Do recognize the difference between an occasional funk and a habit of going off alone and shutting down. The latter could be a sign of depression, being bullied, or even drug use.

Know your child well enough to know the difference!

How I've accomplished this:

Avoid jumping to conclusions

It's often easy for most of us to react—and over-react—to the first few words we hear. If you're too hasty, the words *"I got into a fight at school"* may provoke a harsh response, lots of yelling and grounding your son. But by calmly listening to the whole story, you may learn that he stepped in to protect a younger girl who was being teased and bullied. He may be a hero, rather than a thug!

Even when it's clear that your child was in the wrong, getting all the details first will alleviate any possibility of misjudging the action and the child.

If you quickly jump to conclusions before hearing him out, he may be reluctant to come to you the next time there's an issue he needs to explain. Get the facts.

Just because we're all grown up, doesn't mean we're all-knowing.

How I've accomplished this:

Discuss your problems and solutions

I certainly don't encourage you to "dump" all your problems on your children, but don't try to hide them, either. Children are aware of what goes on, and if they sense that something is wrong, but don't know what, they'll imagine the worst.

In a matter-of-fact way, and without going into a lot of detail, explain your problem, whether it be financial, work-related, or between you and someone else, and then explain how you're handling it. Give the children reason to believe that the problem will be solved. If it's going to affect them (less money for extras, for example), let them know how much of an impact it might have, and how they might help, or be a part of the solution.

By letting your children know you're trying to resolve the problem, you teach them to look for answers to their own problems, rather than depend on others to bail them out.

No matter how bad it seems now ... "This too shall pass."

How I've accomplished this:

Write letters to your child

Sometimes we find it difficult to speak what's in our hearts; especially if a relationship has been strained. But a letter can make a child—even a teenager—feel especially loved. You can put on paper all the feelings you have for them: your pride in their accomplishments, your appreciation for the things they do and say, your love for the person they have become.

You can write notes (at their level of understanding) as soon as they're old enough to read, when they're in their teens and into adulthood. They will treasure them, especially if you have difficulty being able to verbally express your own feelings.

Be sure a letter is a positive thing. Don't write anything that will produce guilt feelings on the child's part, or write of how they may have disappointed you in some way. They probably already know that. Let them know you love them anyway, and praise the things they've done right. They'll be more likely to continue the positive behavior to please you.

Positive feedback breeds positive results

How I've accomplished this:

Leave a little note

While a verbal *"I love you"* or *"Thanks for your help,"* should be given on a regular basis, a written note will be kept, re-read, and treasured. An unexpected note of love, thanks or encouragement, will brighten a child's day when she least expects it. Put a note in her lunch box saying *"I'll be praying for you [or thinking of you] during your test today. I know you'll do well."*

You might give your child a card with a personal note to congratulate her on even a minor achievement ... *"Congratulations on your first A in math!"* Or write a thank you note ... *"I really appreciated your help with the housecleaning on Saturday. You made the house sparkle!"*

And of course, a note left on her bed or slipped into a pocket just to say *"I love you—you fill my life with joy,"* will bring a smile to even the most jaded teen.

Say what you feel, and most importantly, feel what you say.

How I've accomplished this:

Listen attentively

There's nothing more frustrating to a child—or to an adult for that matter—than to be sharing our thoughts or feelings with someone who seems absorbed in another activity.

It's difficult to shift gears from our schedule, chores and priorities and become a patient listener on cue, but that's just what we need to do sometimes. It's important that we stop what we're doing and make *eye contact* while we listen!

Children, especially, need to know that we value what they have to say. Even if it's only excitement over the interesting bug they found, it's important to them. If we're staring at the computer screen and murmur *"That's nice, honey,"* the lack of interest won't be lost on them.

When Shanon comes in upset about the argument she had with her best friend, she really needs you to just listen. Telling her, *"Not now, I'm busy,"* sends the message that her needs are not as important as whatever you happen to be doing at the moment.

But if children believe we're truly interested in what they have to say, no matter how insignificant it may seem to *us*, they'll continue to share their more serious thoughts or problems with us.

If we take the time to give undivided attention to our kids while they talk, we'll reap big dividends in the future … when the issues they'll want to discuss could have a major impact on their lives.

Pay attention now, or pay the price later.

How I've accomplished this:

Understand their point of view

Often, when we're listening, we're already thinking ahead to *our* opinions, thoughts or feelings on a topic. We may be hearing from a parent's point of view, and not understanding that a child sees a situation differently.

Cindy might think the kids at school were making fun of her because they laughed as she walked by. You're thinking their laughter could have been totally unrelated to her. You could be right, but brushing off her problem by telling Cindy she's being over-sensitive won't make her feel any better.

First let her know you understand how she must feel. Then offer one or two other possibilities for their laughter. If you can relate a similar experience in which you believed something and later found out you had been mistaken, share that with her. It could give her hope that she, too, was mistaken. Most importantly, she'll appreciate that you took her concerns seriously, and won't be afraid to tell you about future worries.

Beware of "Listening with your answer running." Hear her out!

How I've accomplished this:

Listen without offering unsolicited advice

When someone is unburdening their problems to us, it's so tempting to jump in and start offering our ideas, opinions, solutions and advice; *"Well, if I were you ..."* Well, we're *not* them, and sometimes a kid just needs to unload, but doesn't want a lecture or advice. They just want a friendly ear; someone who will listen, be understanding, non-judgmental, perhaps even sympathetic. But they don't want the listener to start doling out unwanted advice.

Depending on the problem, the child probably already feels bad about the incident, without having a parent or other adult make him feel worse because he "shoulda" done this or "oughta" have done that. These kinds of unasked-for comments may make him feel like even more of a failure.

When Jimmy says he got a "D" on his spelling test, rather than tell him he should have studied more, you might say, *"I'm sure you feel bad about that, but I bet you can do better next time."* Add a smile and a hug, and you're golden!

Of course, when you're asked for advice or comments, think it through first, be ready, and be gentle.

> *The first duty of love is to listen*   ~ Paul Tillich

How I've accomplished this:

Discuss current events

When bad things happen in the world, children are often confused. Trying to protect them by avoiding discussion is often counter-productive, and could make them feel even more insecure. Be open with your children, tell them what they need to know, but don't offer so much information that they're overwhelmed or more frightened.

Take children's ages into consideration, when discussing news with them. For large scale incidents, such as 9/11, give them reassurance that things will eventually be better again. For less traumatic events that don't directly affect you or your children, let them know that just because a fire, burglary, or other misfortune happened to someone else, that doesn't necessarily mean it will happen to them. Let them know what precautions you've taken against such occurrences. For instance, show them the fire alarms, or the security system, for reassurance.

Depending upon their ages, ask their opinions on what you see in the news; especially events that may affect them in some way, or those that might have a moral lesson attached. You could ask your son how he might have handled a certain situation regarding the environment, for example. But be careful that you're not putting more responsibility on him than he's ready to think about at the time.

Asking your child's opinion or talking to him about these happenings, causes him to think about what's going on in his world, and makes him feel good about being included in the discussion.

The more they understand about the world around them,
the more responsibly they'll act in it.

How I've accomplished this:

Use TV as an opportunity for discussion

There is so much on TV these days that many of us never had to deal with when we were growing up. Imagine the term "water closet" or even the word "pregnant" being cut from a show today, as both were in the sixties! Even very young children are now being exposed to sexual innuendo (and sex itself), violence, and crude language on television—and often in life. It's hard for them to understand why those things are undesirable in real life when they seem so well-accepted and normal on TV shows.

When you see something negative on TV, rather than just change the channel immediately (unless it's extremely violent or disturbing) take the time to discuss what's wrong with it, and why you don't approve. Make it a true discussion—with input from your child—rather than a lecture. By letting them express their opinions, you'll get a feel for how they view the issues, and possibly clear up some misconceptions.

Make it clear that those kinds of shows won't be part of your TV schedule in the future. If necessary, take advantage of the parental control features available.

Every negative influence infiltrating our brain
has a negative impact on our life!

How I've accomplished this:

Ask for their input

Get your children involved in planning a vacation, or let them offer some ideas on how the family as a whole can cut down on expenses. They'll feel like an equal part of the family, rather than just "the kids" who are never listened to. They may surprise you with their thoughts and ideas, and will be more willing to participate in a plan when they've had some direct input.

When our kids were young, we—or they—could call a family meeting at any time to discuss issues. If they called one, they ran it, and were in charge of keeping order. It had the added benefit of building leadership skills!

A family meeting—where everyone has a say—can be a good lesson in working and planning together, discussing problems, and coming up with solutions as a group.

A child who contributes to a solution is more likely to buy into it.

How I've accomplished this:

Don't be too quick to say No

When a child wants to discuss something of importance, perhaps a raise in their allowance, or being permitted to spend the weekend with a friend, have them call a family meeting. (See previous tip.) It'll make them feel as if you really are interested in giving them a fair hearing. Be open-minded, and be willing to offer alternatives if you can't completely agree with their request.

If your 12-year-old daughter wants to wear makeup, suggest she start with a light lipstick this year, and save the eyeshadow for later.

When your 10-year-old son wants to spend all his spare time playing video games, offer a compromise that will allow him 20 minutes of video time for an hour of reading or playing outside.

If you really can't grant their request at all, at least don't close the door completely. Say something like *"I can't agree with that now, but let's discuss it again next month (six months, etc.)"* It leaves the door open, and makes them feel that at least you're taking the request into consideration. When you don't completely negate their choices, but show a willingness to work with them, they'll also be more receptive to accepting a "middle ground."

Of course, this applies to issues that are negotiable. When a request obviously requires a firm "No," for legal or safety reasons, stick to it!

When you respect their requests, they'll be more likely to respect yours.

How I've accomplished this:

Avoid yelling or raising your voice

Having someone yell at us automatically puts us on the defensive. Think about how you'd feel if your boss yelled at you to re-do a report, rather than if he asked you politely to try it again.

A child will probably feel guilty or feel that he's in the wrong when being yelled at, even if he doesn't know why. Then he's more likely to become defensive or argumentative, leading to tempers flaring on both sides.

If he doesn't automatically believe that he must be wrong somehow, he'll at least feel that you're being very unfair, and he'll resent anything you have to say. He might even feel victimized, and that can carry over into other areas of his life. It can all be avoided with a quieter demeanor.

Rather than raising your voice to your son, tell him in a calm manner what is wrong and what needs to be done about it. If you can throw in a "please" along with a smile, all the better.

And while you may think *"Because I said so"* is a good enough reason, it'll sound like a cop-out to a kid. Explaining why is never a bad thing, even if he doesn't agree with your reasoning.

"A gentle answer turns away wrath."   ~ Proverbs 15:1

How I've accomplished this:

~~~~~~~~~~~~~~~~~~~~~~~~~~~~⨂~~~~~~~~~~~~~~~~~~~~~~~~~

EXAMPLE

*Setting an example is not the best means of
influencing another, it is the* only *means.*
~ Albert Einstein

There is great advice for writers, that's even more important in parenting: *show*, don't *tell*. For your child to really grasp values and ethics, you need to show them the way, not just tell them what they "should" do.

Setting an example is one of the best parenting tools we have at our disposal—when used in the right way. But used wrongly, it can be devastating. A segment on the Dr Phil show filmed a little girl alone in her room, talking to her doll, repeating all the negative things her mother constantly said to her. It was sad to listen to. Not only were the words destructive to the child, but she heard them as an example of how to talk to others.

When a child hears his mother tell the ticket seller at the amusement park that Joey is only five years old, when he's actually eight, he'll learn that it's all right to lie and cheat. When he sees his dad take a few grapes in the grocery store and pop them into his mouth, he'll learn that it's okay to steal. And how many times have we heard smokers tell their kids not to smoke, or speeders yell at their teens for having a heavy foot?

But when a child sees Mom return to the clerk the extra $5.00 in change, he'll learn that honesty is the right thing, even when no one else would know the difference.

Make no mistake … your kids will do exactly what you *do*, not just what you *tell* them to do. Make sure you're always setting the best possible example.

"Do as I say, not as I do" is a recipe for disaster - don't follow it!

Admit when you're wrong

One of the best actions we can take to establish credibility with our kids is to admit when we've made a mistake. Maybe we misjudged them, accused them wrongly, or perhaps spoke harshly about another person in error.

If we admit we were wrong and apologize, our kids will learn *first* that no one (not even Dad!) is perfect; and *second*, that it's not the end of the world when they make a mistake. They will understand that they can learn from the mistake, be forgiven if necessary, and move on.

For great examples of this, watch re-runs of the old Andy Griffith show. There are several examples in which Andy misjudged his son Opie in one way or another. By the end of the show, he had realized his mistake, admitted he was wrong, and apologized to the boy.

We are not infallible just because we're adults. If we can admit *our* failures, our kids will be more likely to admit theirs.

An apology is better than a Band-aid for healing hurt feelings.
When you mess up, 'fess up!

How I've accomplished this:

Be willing to change your mind ... if it makes sense

Many parenting experts say we should stick with a decision: that once it has been made, we should never back down. As with any rule, this one sometimes needs to be broken.

There are times when we make a decision based on faulty information or lack of facts. If we later find out things are not as we believed, it's okay to change our minds.

If Jenny begs to go to a school dance, and you say, "No," then later find out it will be completely chaperoned, and Shanon's mom has offered to take them and bring them home, you might decide to let her attend after all.

On the other hand, if you originally said she *could* go, then learned that it was not at the school, but at a club with no chaperones, you should feel justified in changing your mind on that score, also. But this is a tough one, so it's better to get all the facts before making a promise you may have to go back on.

Just make sure you're not backing down from a *good* decision simply because she's whining and begging. If you know your reasons are solid, stick with them. But also be fair and reasonable when circumstances warrant it, rather than hang onto a "That's final!" attitude.

> *Give "Yeses" whenever you feel comfortable,*
> *and they'll respect the "Noes" when they're necessary.*

How I've accomplished this:

Teach courtesy by example, not nagging

I recently saw an older woman give a tired, cranky little girl a lollipop in a store. The Mom then demanded rather loudly, *"Tell her thank you,"* which the little girl dutifully did. The older woman then helped the harried Mom carry her packages to the car, after which the Mom got in, still fussing at her child, and drove off without a word of thanks.

It seems that many young parents want their children to say *please* and *thank you* more to make the *parents* look good, than to learn any real lesson. If *you* don't show courtesy and good manners to others, it'll be very difficult for your children to grasp that they should do it on a regular basis, not just when Mom or Dad yells at them to do so. Set the example by saying *please* and *thank you* to your children at the dinner table, when they do a chore, or whenever the situation merits it.

> *A good example has twice the value of good advice.*
> ~ Author Unknown

How I've accomplished this:

Speak only positive things about others

Children learn from what they hear, see and experience. If they hear you gossiping about the neighbors, or complaining about the "jerks" on the road, they'll also be quick to criticize and resort to name calling.

Keep your comments positive. Even if you have a legitimate gripe about someone, don't voice it in front of the kids; or if you're in a situation where it can't be avoided, be sure you only criticize the person's actions, not the individual. For example, if the dry-cleaner lost your best jacket, try to settle it in a mature manner.

Yelling *"What kind of idiots are you that can't hang onto a jacket!"* in front of your child, is *not* setting a good example. A better response would be a calm *"How do you plan to make this right?"* Not only will your child learn how to respond to difficulties, but the dry-cleaner will probably be more willing to fix the problem if you're reasonable.

If you don't control your temper and your words, little Joey will take every demeaning name he hears and eventually hurl them at someone else. Avoid name-calling at all costs. It's just not necessary, and it doesn't accomplish anything.

If you can't speak kindly about another, then say nothing.

How I've accomplished this:

Watch your language

One of the most discouraging declines over the past couple of decades is the language around us. Certain four-letter words were never uttered in the presence of a lady. Now I hear the "ladies" themselves hurling these words at their mates, co-workers, and children.

If you are constantly cursing others and using foul language, of course your children will do the same. You might *tell* them not to (sometimes swearing as you do so,) but they'll be so accustomed to hearing bad language that your message will have no meaning to them. Even if they don't use offensive words in front of you, they will when they're with their friends.

If your language is always civil, however, your children will respect that—at least in your presence—and probably away from you as well. We did not even allow the words "shut up" to be used in our family, and to this day, neither of the kids use that phrase. (And my then-thirty-year-old son once apologized to me for having to use the word "damn" in the context of telling me a story! We may have gone overboard in our training!)

Before choosing your words,
   think about how they'll sound coming from your child's mouth!

How I've accomplished this:

Provide good role models

Of course *you* are a good role model for your children, especially after reading this book! But help them to see other *real* people as individuals to look up to. Most kids worship celebrities and sports figures as their heroes. Some deserve the hero worship; most do not. But your kids may not notice that the next-door neighbor mows the lawn for the elderly couple down the street, or that the teenager who babysits them also volunteers at a child crisis center.

Make sure the people in your child's life are those who provide a good example and influence, whether family, friends, neighbors, their friends' parents, etc. Point out how these people—whether adults or older children—help those around them, speak well of others, or even perform occasional random acts of kindness.

On the flip side, whenever possible, avoid those individuals whose actions and attitudes send the wrong message. We can't shelter our children from all the negative influences in life, but we can provide the very best alternatives to counteract them.

Real heroes are just ordinary people doing extraordinary things.

How I've accomplished this:

Share a Sense of Humor

Humor works. And humor is contagious. A good sense of humor, even during tense or stressful times, can do a world of good. It can elevate your mood and get your day off to a good start. Let your children see you laugh and kid around. Let them know it's okay to have fun. Use humor to tease them out of a bad mood. Just make sure you're not teasing in the wrong way, which could hurt feelings and make them even grumpier.

Humor helps you keep a positive outlook even in tough situations. If you look for humor in all circumstances, and laugh when little things go wrong, you'll be showing your child that you don't fall apart at the least little annoyance, or even the bigger problems.

A good sense of humor has the added benefit of reducing stress, increasing energy levels, and has even been shown to boost the immune system.

When your child tries her own brand of humor, even if it's corny, make an effort to appreciate it. It won't cost you anything to laugh at her riddles and jokes, and it will help build self-confidence.

> *Begin each day with humor,*
> *and the rest of the day will be easier to take.*

How I've accomplished this:

DISCIPLINE

"Beyond a wholesome discipline, be gentle with yourself.
You are a child of the universe, no less than the trees or the
stars; you have a right to be here. ~ Desiderata

The word "discipline" often has a negative connotation, because—especially in the eyes of a child—punishment is often involved. But to discipline a child actually means to instruct him in a code of conduct that will help him grow to be a responsible adult.

Discipline can include praise, criticism, feedback, and yes … punishment.

Praise is a great disciplinary tool! When you catch your kids doing something right, praise them for it, and they'll be more likely to want to repeat that behavior.

As far as punishment goes, that's something you'll need to determine for yourselves. I'm not here to comment on the spank/no-spank debate. But some of the tips in this section touch on viable options and ways to handle punishment.

Criticism is telling your daughter what she did wrong, while feedback is telling her how she could do it better. They might both accomplish the same thing, but the recipient will feel much better, and be more willing to comply when given feedback rather than criticism.

Learning the difference between the two, and applying feedback more often, can go a long way toward having more constructive and respectful conversations with your child. Several of the tips in this section provide examples of using feedback instead of criticism. Try it and see what a difference it can make.

Compliment often

Always look for ways to compliment your child. Whether Jenny was on time for the school bus, or hung up her clothes without being told, compliment and thank her as soon as you notice. Positive reinforcement is the best way to prolong good behavior. All of us love compliments and children thrive on it. Try to gear compliments toward those areas where they have control. Better to compliment her for how well she brushed her hair and dressed herself, than to simply say she looks pretty. Better to compliment her good study habits than to just tell her she's smart for getting an "A" on her test.

One caution: don't praise and compliment so often, and so generally, that it becomes meaningless. Constantly telling Jenny that she is "wonderful" or "super" doesn't really say anything, and it begins to lose its magic after a while. Praise specific actions or attributes, and she'll take you more seriously.

A sincere compliment will always go further than any criticism.

How I've accomplished this:

Be relaxed, but always be in charge

There's a difference between being lenient and being lax. You don't want to be a super-strict disciplinarian, but nor do you want to be so lax that your daughter doesn't know what the ground rules are—or even if there *are* rules.

In your relationship with her, be casual, easily approachable, and friendly. But when there are rules to be followed, be in charge and make sure your standards are adhered to.

Kids need to know you care. When I was fifteen, I had a friend who—when I asked what her curfew was—said *"I don't have one. My parents don't care how late I stay out."* It was obvious from her tone of voice and expression that this wasn't something she was happy about. She might still have argued over a curfew, but by having one, at least she'd know her parents cared about her.

It's possible to be so laid-back that your child thinks you're not interested in what they do, and they'll take advantage of that. Make sure they understand that many of the standards you set are because you care about them and the choices they're making. Put it all in terms of love, and they'll be more likely to accept your decisions.

Rules made from love rather than power are more easily accepted.

How I've accomplished this:

Praise character, as well as actions

It's easy to praise actions—those things we see our child do—but it's a little more difficult sometimes to point out good character traits; those areas that will determine the kind of human being he will be as he grows in adulthood. If you only praise Jody for his good grades and hard work, he'll think he has to constantly be an achiever to earn your praise or respect.

If Jody broke your favorite vase, and admitted to it right away, compliment him for his honesty. When you're feeling tired or ill, and he gives you a spontaneous hug, praise his compassion. Tell him how thoughtful he is when he shares his toy with another.

Without a lot of preaching and explaining, you will be teaching him how to be a caring, compassionate adult.

One taste of praise is worth more than a mouthful of lecture.

How I've accomplished this:

Offer suggestions in a positive way

Life is filled with "Don'ts" and children seem to hear them more than anyone. *"Don't get dirty," "Don't let go of the kite," "Don't run into the street"* and on and on. If you find yourself saying "don't" too often, take a minute to try and rephrase the request in a positive way.

Studies have shown that the brain doesn't process the word "don't." When you say *"Don't get dirty"* the brain hears *"Get dirty."* Restating the request in a positive way will be more likely to get positive results.

In the above examples, you could say, *"Try to stay clean," "Hold the kite tightly,"* and *"Please stay in the yard."* The end result (if obeyed) is exactly the same—a clean kid clinging to a kite inside the yard—but the child doesn't get the feeling that he's not allowed to do *anything.*

If you can say the same thing with either a "Do"or a "Don't"…
always go for the "Do"

How I've accomplished this:

If you must criticize—make it constructive

If you begin your criticism, *"Why do you always ...,"* you've already put your child in a defensive mode and lost the battle. He won't hear anything else you say; including the actions you want him to change.

Instead, offer a suggestion of a better way to do something, and whenever possible, show how the better way can benefit him. For example (in a pleasant tone of voice,) *"Connor, if you give your room a quick pick-up before you go to bed each night, you won't have to spend Saturday morning cleaning, and you'll have more time to play."*

Be careful in your use of the word "should" as well. Rather than tell a child what he *should* do, just discuss it as if it's a done deal. Instead of saying *"You should clean your room before we leave"* try saying, *"After your room is clean, we'll go."* This assumes that he will clean the room.

Also avoid words like *always, never, just,* or *only,* (if you would just ..., would only ..., you never ...) these words have a connotation that suggests the idea is so simple they should have thought of it themselves. You might as well be saying *"Any dummy knows to ...."*

A pleasant voice + neutral words + benefit = more cooperation.

How I've accomplished this:

Criticize the act – not the child

"Why are you always so sloppy? Why must you always leave the bathroom such a mess?" Statements like this will only serve to make your child feel badly about herself and think that she can't do any better. Besides, you're asking a question—even if rhetorical—for which there is no right answer, which puts her in a losing situation.

Phrase your criticism in a way that says it's the messy bathroom you disapprove of—not the child. *"Would you please make an effort to leave the bathroom neater when you finish your shower?"* is a direct request, not a criticism of her, personally.

This also goes back to the unconditional love mentioned earlier. When you criticize the child, she might worry that you don't love her, or even like her. Criticizing the behavior does not present that same fear, especially if you follow your request with, *"I love you!"*

"I may not like what you do, but I love who you are."

How I've accomplished this:

Use **I,** *not* **You** *statements*

Using the same bathroom scenario as in the previous example, present your statement from the point of view of how *you* feel about it, rather than *her* failures. For instance, instead of saying, *"You are so messy,"* you might say, *"I really don't like coming into the bathroom and having wet towels on the floor and toothpaste all over the countertop. I'd appreciate having it left neater for me."*

Then make sure she understands exactly what "neater" means to you: towels hung up, dirty clothes in hamper, counter top wiped off, etc.

Beginning a statement with the word "You" generally puts the other person on the defensive before they even hear the rest of the sentence. *"You always ..."* is even worse, and it serves to make the child feel guilty about their actions. Guilt is not a parenting tool. Just as you should not be "guilted" into doing something, nor should you use guilt to intimidate a child.

When you use "I," or state the objection from your point of view, it's not about what *they* are doing wrong, it's about *your* reaction to it, or what you would like to see changed.

Using 'I' instead of 'You' is a small thing, but it makes a big difference in how the request is heard and perceived.

Correction does much, but encouragement does more.
~ Johann Wolfgang von Goethe

How I've accomplished this:

Define limits and expectations

The mother of three-year old Kellen told him to put his dirty socks in the hamper. She came back later and they were on the bed. She told him again, and after checking back, saw that they were in the dresser. She scolded him, and told him more strongly to put them in the hamper. He looked up at her in tears and said *"Mommy, what's a hamper?"*

Children learn their vocabulary as they go, and we often forget they may not understand some of the words we use. Or they may have another idea of its meaning. The word "clean," for instance, has one meaning to you and a completely different meaning to a three-year old—or even a 13-year-old! Instead of just saying, *"Clean your room,"* tell him to put toys away and put dirty clothes in the hamper (after explaining what a hamper is!) He'll be more likely to understand exactly what you want from him.

When you explain terminology, scope, and limits involved in any instruction, you'll get better results. You might have the child repeat what he heard, or you might ask questions to determine if he understands the words you're using. If you're not sure, show him exactly what you mean.

They can't obey the rules if they don't understand the terms.

How I've accomplished this:

45

Discipline calmly, not in anger

Displaying anger towards a child—especially a young one—can make her feel that she is a bad person, or worse, that her parents don't love her. A calm punishment, with an explanation as to why she is being punished, sends the message that it is her *behavior* that is unacceptable, not *her*. Make sure she knows exactly why she is being punished, and what kind of behavior you expect from her in the future.

When you discipline, bend down to her level. Adults are intimidating enough just being so much taller; when they're tall *and* angry, it compounds the child's fear. Get on her level, and speak calmly, but firmly.

Then end the discussion or time-out with a hug and the words "*I love you*" to reassure her of your love and commitment to her.

Great anger is more destructive than the sword. ~ Tamil proverb

How I've accomplished this:

Replace scolding with requests

Since we're the adults, we sometimes take advantage of the ability to nag, scold, and belittle our children. We wouldn't dream of treating a guest the same way. Instead of yelling, *"Don't leave the dirty glass on the table!"* simply say, *"Please put that in the dishwasher."* It achieves the same result, but without making the child feel as though they've messed up yet again.

And when you catch them putting the glass in the dishwasher without being told, be sure to praise them, or at least say, *"Thanks —I appreciate that!"*

A "Thank You"along with a smile will go a long way toward making the desired action become habit. As an added benefit, it sets the good example of using "Please" and "Thank You," even to family members!

> *Kids are people too, and appreciate being treated*
> *with kindness and respect.*

How I've accomplished this:

Avoid negative labels

One of the worst and most damaging things we can do is use negative labels to describe our child's behavior or actions. To tell a child she is lazy, stupid, irresponsible, or clumsy does nothing to help change her poor behavior. In fact, it is more likely to reinforce it! At all costs, avoid labeling the child with negative terms.

If you're going to use labels, look for the good attributes and behaviors, and find the words to describe those. Remember to focus on the areas they can control.

While telling your son he is handsome or cute won't hurt him, and will probably boost his self-esteem a bit, it won't give him a sense of having contributed toward it. But if you tell him he's clever for having figured out how to fix his bike, you're complimenting his skill, problem-solving abilities and persistence —attributes that he can control and strengthen.

There is never a justification for using a negative label.

How I've accomplished this:

Determine your discipline style

It's tough enough for a kid to understand what's right and wrong, without being caught in the middle of her parents' interpretations of those values. If Dad believes in spanking, but Mom is from the "time out" school of discipline, there are bound to be clashes.

If Mom says the beds have to be made every morning, no matter what, and Dad says don't worry about it—what's a kid gonna do? Well, she's probably not going to make the bed. Then Mom's on her case again.

If these kinds of battles are going on regularly, it's time to sit down and make some decisions. Each parent needs to be able to give up some of his or her disciplinary values. Dad could stop spanking if Mom will ease up on the bed-making routine. Whatever the decisions are, the two of you have to agree, or the child will play each of you against the other.

When parents disagree, the child will run amok.

How I've accomplished this:

Be consistent with discipline

Besides agreeing on disciplinary tactics, another critical factor is consistency. If, when Bobby comes in after curfew, you look the other way one time, but then ground him the next, he won't know what to think. If you make a rule, enforce it. Every time ... with a*lmost* no exceptions.

I say almost, because sometimes unavoidable things do happen. If he's late because of a flat tire, and you have evidence of that—he doesn't deserve to be punished. But if he says he ran out of gas, even if it's true—too bad. If he's old enough to drive, he's old enough to read a gas gauge and take precautions against running out.

Be fair, be firm, and be consistent.

How I've accomplished this:

Avoid over-reacting to minor infractions

You are not going to have a perfect kid! Get used to the idea now, and accept the fact that she will fail, make mistakes, break dishes, leave wet towels on the floor, and forget to feed the cat. These are *not* major flaws in her character!

If you scream at her, or punish her severely for these types of misdeeds, then later, when you need to get on her case for something really big (sneaking out, taking the car at 14 and knocking over a lamp post,) it won't seem any more wrong to her than the wet towel on the floor.

It's okay—and often necessary—to ask her to be more careful with the dishes, tell her to pick up the towel, and remind her to feed the cat, just be careful not to go overboard.

If you over-react now, you'll lose credibility later.

How I've accomplished this:

Be careful when reacting to the unexpected

Whether it's the question, *"Mommy, what does sex mean?"* the statement, *"Mom, I'm pregnant,"* or anything in between, try to stay calm and not get flustered. This can be extremely difficult, but is crucial to maintaining clear and open communication.

If necessary, take a deep breath and excuse yourself for a few minutes to think through the problem. Remind yourself that nothing is so bad that it can't be handled in some way. There are solutions to every problem, but you can't discover or discuss them if you're not thinking clearly. Once you've had a few minutes alone, you'll be more prepared to face the problem. When you return, you'll be able to discuss it in a calm and rational manner. You will feel better, and so will your child.

If you demonstrate early on that you can take tough news or questions without freaking out, you'll earn your children's trust when the big issues come along. They'll know they can come to you and you won't fall apart, scream at them, or become hysterical.

Nothing is insurmountable when love and faith are involved.

How I've accomplished this:

Make the punishment fit the offense

If Rachel continues watching TV long after you've asked her to do a chore, grounding her for a week is pretty extreme. On the other hand, if she took your expensive camera without permission and broke it, taking away her dessert is not strong enough to teach her right from wrong.

Whenever possible, relate the punishment to the infraction in some way. In the first instance, you could take away Rachel's TV privileges for the rest of the day, or have her do the dusting in that room the next couple of times. In the case of the broken camera, she should be made to pay all or part of the cost of repairing or replacing it—which could be an expensive prospect.

Think about how serious the infraction is, and do not punish beyond what it deserves, but do punish to the full extent of what it deserves.

Actions have consequences. Wrong actions have strong consequences.

How I've accomplished this:

Choose your battles

Don't stress over whether Sage eats all his peas, or Sadie wears blue socks with the red dress. Decide what's really important and stick to those issues.

If you make a rule, enforce it; but don't make so many rules that it's impossible to obey all of them. Ease up on the minor things, such as what they must eat (as long as they're getting the nutrition they need) or wear, (as long as they're decently covered) and how much order is required in their room (as long as the health department doesn't need to intervene.)

Focus on the battles of character, rather than of chores. It's better to insist they be honest and responsible than that their bed is made or their clothes match.

If you go easy on these inconsequential matters, the more critical ones like homework, hygiene, and honesty will be easier to enforce.

Sometimes, the outcome doesn't justify the battle.

How I've accomplished this:

ENCOURAGEMENT

"The more I encourage my child to think for himself,
the more he will care what I think."
~ Author Unknown

The words "praise" and "encouragement" are sometimes used interchangeably. However, praise usually takes the form of kind words given for something already done, and encouragement is helping a person to do or be something in the present or future. Encouragement can also be used after a failure, to build up morale.

While discipline, criticism, feedback, and other forms of correction all do their part in changing a child's behavior, encouragement will go much farther toward attaining the desired goal.

William Arthur Ward said, *"Flatter me and I may not believe you. Criticize me, and I may not like you. Ignore me, and I may not forgive you. Encourage me, and I will not forget you …."*

And it's true; we always remember the people who have encouraged us along our way in life. Next to love, encouragement is the greatest gift you can give your child.

Encourage new experiences

While insisting he finish every bite of the liver isn't going to win you any points, encouraging Freddie to at least taste the strawberry yogurt could have a surprising result. It's easy for children and adults alike to get into a rut of doing the same old thing, the same old way. Offer a variety of experiences to your children, but don't force any one thing on them.

While driving in the car, you could play CDs of different types of music: classical, country, Cajun … whatever you don't normally listen to. Encourage them to actually listen, rather than just dismiss it without a fair chance. My children learned to love Ravel's Bolero and Simon & Garfunkel equally because we played a variety of music on the trips back and forth to school.

If you always go to a park on a Saturday, try a museum next time. They don't have to like it, but they should experience different activities so at least they'll *know* they don't like it—and even if they won't admit they like it now, it may plant a seed for the future. And when *they* want to try new things—be supportive as far as is practical.

Trying new adventures and experiences builds confidence.

How I've accomplished this:

Help develop skills and talents

Children will go through a lot of "wannabe's" while trying to find out what they enjoy or are good at. Within reason, help them explore various interests to discover their skills, talents and desires. Then encourage them to follow through on the commitment and responsibilities involved.

Recognize that they will acquire and lose interest in a wide variety of activities as they grow and mature, and you may not be able to finance all their desires: pianos, drums, dance lessons and costumes, sports equipment—can all be very expensive!

But encouraging them to explore their interests, and making them responsible for some of the cost, will help determine where their hearts lie, and what they're willing to sacrifice for their dreams. The more *they're* willing to invest, the stronger their interest probably is, and the more they will appreciate it.

> *Make sure it's* their *dream, not* yours,
> *that you're helping them pursue.*

How I've accomplished this:

Encourage them to read

Reading can increase knowledge and fuel new interests in the world around us. If your youngster doesn't like to read, find out if there is a problem with his ability. It's possible that he doesn't enjoy it because he has to struggle. If dyslexia, poor vision, or a learning disability is a problem, it's important to find out early.

If there is no problem, but still no desire, get involved in reading together. You might start by pointing out an article that's related to his hobby, or by helping him find books that appeal to his interests. If he's a huge basketball fan, show him the wide variety of books—fiction, biographies, history, statistics—that will help him learn more about the sport. You might also recommend books that you enjoyed at his age, and describe why you liked them so much.

Show him the sections in libraries and bookstores where books in his particular field of interest are, and help him select a few appropriate for his age. If you also read the books, you can discuss them with him. He'll probably think you're pretty cool if you can rattle off some facts about his favorite players, for instance, and you'll have yet another way to build rapport.

The child who reads has the whole world open to him.

How I've accomplished this:

Teach goal-setting

Even young children can set goals and reach them. When you encourage them along the way, then help them feel the satisfaction of reaching the goal, you will set them on a life-long path of goal-setting and help them become consistent achievers.

Help young children set goals you know they can reach, but let them do it on their own, with encouragement—but no help—from you. For instance, a six-year-old who receives a $1.00 week allowance, could set a goal to have saved a certain amount of money by her birthday.

Or, if you're from the "Gold Star" school of rewards, have your child set a goal to have earned 10 gold stars by the end of the week, for chores done or for good behavior. A goal for older children could be reading a certain number of books each month, getting at least two "A"s each semester, or whatever is important to them and appropriate for their age.

Keep in mind, the *child* should set the goal, and reach it on his own, in order for it to be meaningful. You can offer ideas on how to attain it, or steps to take, but you shouldn't do it for them. Your role is to encourage and praise.

A child who sees a string of successes, will grow in confidence.

How I've accomplished this:

Encourage when they're down

When we feel at our lowest—like a failure, like nobody loves us, or that we just can't do anything right—that's when we need the most encouragement. Children feel this even more acutely, because they don't have the experience to know that "this too shall pass."

When Dave is feeling down in the dumps, he doesn't want to be told to "get over it" or that "things will be better tomorrow."

Simple reassurance that he is not the awful, unlovable person he imagines himself to be at the time, will go a long way toward lifting him back up. Encourage him to look at all the good things he has going for him, but *do not* negate the event or problem that has brought him down. Whatever issue he's dealing with is very important to him.

Telling Dave it's "nothing" won't make him feel any better, and may give him the impression that you just don't understand or care.

Help your child to see *all* sides to whatever has him feeling blue, not just the negative view he's seeing at the time.

A word of encouragement during a failure is worth more
than an hour of praise after success. ~ Author Unknown

How I've accomplished this:

Know the difference between encouraging and coercing

We sometimes think we're offering encouragement, when what we're really doing is nagging. There's a fine line between the two.

If you're not sure which role you're playing, ask yourself, "*Is this his goal I'm encouraging, or something I want him to do?*"

When a friend was teaching his son Johnny to play tennis, the dad was constantly criticizing his style. Johnny got frustrated and was close to giving up. Dad was hoping his son would become a professional player, while Johnny just wanted to have fun with the game.

Keep in mind that it's encouragement if you're helping with an activity he wants to excel at and he appreciates your comments.

It's coercion if he just wants to have fun and you're pushing too hard or being overly critical.

Understand the difference and bite your tongue when necessary.

How I've accomplished this:

~~~~~~~~~~~~~~~~~~~~~~~~~~~~~~)(~~~~~~~~~~~~~~~~~~~~~~~~~~

PEOPLE BUILDING

Act as if what you do makes a difference. It does!
~ William James

People Building: the act of building up other human beings, rather than cutting them down.

The great thing about People Building is that it needn't cost anything. It's as simple as saying kind, encouraging words, helping others in need, giving compliments, praising positive behavior, volunteering, and practicing Random Acts of Kindness. Anything done to make other people feel better about themselves, or to lighten their load, is People Building.

And anyone can do it! The younger a child begins his People Building career, the more likely he is to become a caring, confident, responsible adult.

All the tips in this section are People Building opportunities—for you *and* your child!

~~~~~~~~~~~~~~~~~~~~~~~~~~~~)(~~~~~~~~~~~~~~~~~~~~~~~~

Demonstrate charitable acts

If you've volunteered to serve Thanksgiving dinner at a shelter this year, invite the older children to join you. Or get the younger ones involved in helping you gather toys for a children's hospital. Even if they don't want to participate now, seeing you help others will plant a seed for future work.

Something as simple as taking a meal to a neighbor who is just home from the hospital can show your child that sharing and looking out for others is a part of being responsible and compassionate. Let them help with the meal, perhaps putting the cookies on a plate, or writing a note. Then have them go with you to the neighbor's home.

Young children may see volunteering as just another chore— something they have to do for someone else. They don't get "what's in it for them." Be sure to express often the good feelings that you gain from the experience. Have them go along with you a couple of times, even if they don't want to join in, and help them find the benefit.

No act of kindness, no matter how small, is ever wasted. ~ Aesop

How I've accomplished this:

Encourage volunteering in their field of interest

It's easier to volunteer in an area where you already have some interest. Analyze your children's pursuits, hobbies, and passions, and look for places where they might volunteer. Have them go online to look for opportunities in your community.

If your teenager loves babysitting, she might decide to volunteer at a child crisis center. If your son enjoys working in the yard, he might want to help with landscaping at a low-income development. If crocheting is your daughter's passion, she can make afghans for nursing homes or homeless shelters.

There is always something that needs to be done, and there's always someone—even a youngster—who can do it.

> *If you have much, give of your wealth;*
> *if you have little, give of your heart.*
> ~ Arabian Proverb

How I've accomplished this:

Include others in activities

People building is not just intended for the extremely needy. You can demonstrate this by inviting a lonely neighbor to join you for dinner, or by taking an elderly friend to the mall with you. Let your kids see that sharing time is also a way to help others.

Maybe your son's friend from school, whose single mom can't afford many extras, could use some fun.

By encouraging your son to include his friend in your family's trip to the water park, you're teaching him to be aware of the circumstances of those around him, and to reach out and help whenever possible. He'll see the value of sharing and including others, and will realize that lightening the load of another does not always involve hard work.

As an added benefit, you may have provided a much-needed boost of confidence to the other youngster.

> *It's easy to make a buck.*
> *It's a lot tougher to make a difference.*
> ~ Tom Brokaw

How I've accomplished this:

Practice Random Acts of Kindness

Most parents practice random acts of kindness on their children on a daily basis, without even trying. It's what parents do—who we are.

But sometimes we do something extra nice and unexpected, like picking up a new book they've been wanting, or making their favorite dessert even when *we're* on a diet.

While we don't normally announce our good deeds to others, it wouldn't hurt to leave a little note with the book or dessert saying "A *random act of kindness for you. Pass it on.*" Then let them figure out what they can do for someone else—not you—to make that person's day better. If their very next act of kindness is for you, it becomes a "payback" type situation—not random at all. However, once they understand the concept, they'll be doing nice things for you just because they want to.

It's fine to praise your child when you see him do a random act of kindness, but don't go overboard with it. If he's *always* praised, the "random act" might then become something to do just for the payback.

In about the same degree as you are helpful, you will be happy.
~ Karl Reiland

How I've accomplished this:

Encourage sharing

Teach your child very early on how to share with others. If little Timmy has difficulty with the concept of giving up his red truck to another playmate, you might have them exchange toys, so Timmy can have something new to play with while his friend plays with the truck. Teaching children how to share when they're young sets the stage for them to share with others as they get older.

Eventually this sharing can take the form of giving, rather than loaning, when they willingly give up some of their toys for a homeless shelter or donate some of their allowance to a disaster relief fund. If you start early and encourage regularly, giving and sharing will become life-long habits.

The transition from sharing little red trucks
to sharing with the Red Cross will be an easy leap!

How I've accomplished this:

Teach Gratitude

Every child should be taught to write thank you notes as soon as they can form a few letters. Even if it's only a few scrawled words saying "Thank you, Nana," it's a start. You might want to establish a rule that the child cannot wear, eat, play with or spend a gift until the thank you note has been written. That will get them moving!

The best way to teach gratitude is by example. If they see that you are thankful for having a car that runs, instead of constantly complaining that it's not the newest model, they will begin to understand the concept of gratitude. Find little ways to get the message across to them. Whenever you catch yourself starting to make a negative comment, look instead for the positive in the situation. Rather than say, "I hate doing the laundry," try, "Isn't it great that we have such nice clothes to wear!"

Try to always show gratitude to the people in your life, and encourage your kids to do the same. Set the example by expressing thanks for the little things they do.

> *"Kind words can be short and easy to speak,*
> *but their echoes are truly endless."*
> ~ Mother Teresa of Calcutta

How I've accomplished this:

RESPECT

A child who is allowed to be disrespectful to his parents
will not have true respect for anyone.
~ Billy Graham

Many of the tips in this book lead to respect: listening, paying attention, respecting opinions, etc.

It has been said we should treat guests like family, and our family like guests. It makes sense if you think about it. Ask yourself if you would scream at a guest to close the door behind them, or speak to them in a sarcastic manner. Probably not.

It all boils down to treating your child with the same respect as you would treat a co-worker, neighbor, or anyone else you hold in high esteem. And no one deserves higher esteem than our own family!

Respect for those who are different

Respecting diversity should not mean pretending we're all the same. Trying to act as if there are no differences among people will simply confuse a child. Instead, address the differences, whether they be of race, religion, shape, size, color, or physical or mental challenges.

Explain to your child that every single individual is different from every other. Some differences may be as simple as color of hair, or an abundance of freckles. Point out differences between your child and his best friend, and how each of them have things they're good at, and things they're not so good at, but they are both worthy of being treated the same, and treated with respect.

While it's not necessary to *focus* on differences, acknowledging they exist is more honest than pretending we're all exactly alike.

No matter what the differences,
everyone deserves equal treatment and equal respect.

How I've accomplished this:

Gender Respect

A healthy respect between the genders is an important part of helping kids to love and respect themselves. In these days of equality and political correctness, it's a bit tricky to know what you can say or do to another—especially those of the opposite sex. A male hugging a female could be taken as just a friendly hug … or sexual harassment. A woman hugging a male friend might be seen as just showing affection … or flirting.

It's important that everyone respect everyone else, regardless of sex, race, religion or other differences. But we also need to teach our kids to show respect to—and demand respect from—the opposite sex.

Long before they become teenagers, boys should learn that women are individuals to be valued, not sexual objects to be snickered at and treated as possessions.

Girls need to understand that guys aren't toys to be played with, manipulated, or treated with contempt.

Learning these lessons early on will help kids relate better to the opposite sex when they reach dating age.

Treat the opposite sex with respect,
and relationships will go more smoothly.

How I've accomplished this:

Respect their personal space

Once kids reach a certain age, they're embarrassed just being *seen* with their parents. When we do something we think is funny or cute, it only magnifies their humiliation. While they're going through this stage it's better that we just become invisible when their friends are around. Even trying to "be cool" and fit in with their crowd can backfire. They'd rather we be parents than pals in that situation.

Younger kids don't mind being with us, but they still don't like us saying or doing things that draw attention to them.

And of course, the worst thing we can do is talk about them to others, while in their presence. Even saying something seemingly harmless, like "he's shy," or "he hates his new haircut," can make a child feel there's something wrong with him, and cause embarrassment. And it can have the unwanted effect of reinforcing the very trait—shyness, for example—you want him to overcome.

> *You've got to know when to hug 'em,*
> *know when to kiss 'em, and know when to walk away.*

How I've accomplished this:

Treat their friends with respect

Sometimes we just don't quite like the kid our son has befriended. Perhaps the boy comes from a different background or economic status than we do, or maybe he has shifty eyes, a nose ring, or a punk haircut.

But unless we know something specific about this friend, that we think may be a bad influence, we should not make assumptions or jump to conclusions about his personality, character traits, or prison record. If we treat him with respect, he'll probably respect us. If we make an effort to get to know him, we may just discover a really nice kid behind those shifty eyes!

Obviously, if the kid in question is a true troublemaker, drag racer, drug user, or worse, and you honestly don't want your son hanging out with him, you need to be the parent and put an end to the relationship.

But this tip isn't about that kind of kid; it's about the ones we just might have formed an unwarranted prejudice against.

And remember, your kids may not like all of your friends either!

How I've accomplished this:

Insist that your kids respect you

While it's fine for your offspring to feel comfortable enough with you to speak their mind, kid around, and give you a friendly punch on the arm, don't allow that to disintegrate to the point where they're talking back, cursing at you, or inflicting any type of abuse; verbal or physical.

If you allow them to talk back at an early age, it will continue as they get older, and by the time they're teenagers, there will be no turning back. Even a toddler can learn what you will and will not tolerate. A short time-out followed by an explanation that it is not okay to call Daddy a poopy-head, should do the trick.

Demand respect from them, and they'll appreciate it in the long run. Since you will be giving them respect, they will appreciate that and reciprocate.

No matter how much they may act otherwise,
your kids want boundaries, not buddies.

How I've accomplished this:

Stand by your child

Don't let others—of *any* age—bully your kids or talk negatively about them. Friends or neighbors not as enlightened in building self-esteem as you are, may want to tease your child about a weakness or shortcoming. They may think it's funny to call him "shrimp," but it may be hurtful to Bobby. If your son sees that you're allowing this to go on, he may believe that you agree with the neighbor's assessment of him. Insist that your friends and peers respect your kids.

This is not to say you should jump in and take over your child's issues with children his age, but you should defend him against those older or bigger than he is, or who might intimidate him.

Nor should you defend him when he has obviously done something wrong, and he needs to take responsibility for it. But *do* let your child know you'll support him against others who want to hurt him.

Your unwavering support is a huge confidence builder!

How I've accomplished this:

Avoid comparing your child to anyone else

It's not unusual for a parent to compare one of their children to another, but such comparisons should be avoided—especially within either child's hearing. Those comments can be unsettling and demeaning, especially if one child believes that the other is better than she is in some way. It's even worse if she thinks that you actually favor the other child. (And who hasn't heard *"Mom always liked you best!"*?)

Kids have enough self-esteem problems without being compared to others, or asked *"Why can't you get all 'A's like John?"* or *"If you'd just practice more, you could play piano as well as Jen."* Don't compound their insecurities by making unfair comparisons.

Every child is an individual, with his or her own strengths and weaknesses. To expect one to be as good or talented as another is unfair, and will not make it any easier for them to achieve their potential. They'll always feel like they're letting you down in some way.

Let your child be who she is; strengths, weaknesses, and all.

How I've accomplished this:

~~~~~~~~~~~~~~~~~~~~~~~~~~~~~~~⨝~~~~~~~~~~~~~~~~~~~~~~~~

RESPONSIBILITY

The willingness to accept responsibility for one's own life
is the source from which self-respect springs.
~ Joan Didion

There is probably no more important lesson you can teach a child than to be responsible; for themselves, their chores, their money, and for caring about others. I've seen kids who have skated through life never being held accountable for their actions, nor having any responsibility. Those children became adults who were incapable of holding a job, paying their bills, taking care of themselves and their possessions, or knowing how to get along in life.

A good friend was put in a foster home on a farm when he was six. He was treated well and was taught to be responsible for the animals and to do his part to help the family, until he left at age eighteen.

Today, in his eighties, he credits those lessons in responsibility for helping him become an extremely successful businessman and entrepreneur, as well as someone who is highly respected for his caring and responsible nature.

A child who learns responsibility early on, can do just about anything with the rest of his life.

Train up a child in the way he should go,
and when he is old he will not depart from it.
~ Proverbs 22:6

~~~~~~~~~~~~~~~~~~~~~~~~~~~~~~⨝~~~~~~~~~~~~~~~~~~~~~~~~

Give a child responsibility

Give your children easy chores early on, and increase their responsibilities as they grow. Even small children can handle jobs such as matching socks from the laundry, picking up their toys, and putting clothes in the laundry hamper. My three-year-old grandson could easily fold the dish towels and wash cloths, and enjoyed doing it! Older children can prepare easy meals, mow the lawn, empty the trash, and more.

One of the best lessons a child can learn is to put things back where they belong. If he learns this early on, it'll eliminate a lot of the frustration of looking for things later in life. He will be gaining organizational skills, along with learning to respect the property of others.

If their jobs are presented as an *expectation*, not an *option*, most kids will eventually realize it's an everyday part of family life, and their particular jobs will become a matter of habit.

Remind them that the way they handle responsibility now, determines how you will trust them to handle it in the future, when they will want more rights and freedom. Reinforce that their current actions may determine their future limits!

If you want children to keep their feet on the ground,
put some responsibility on their shoulders.
~ Abigail Van Buren

How I've accomplished this:

Play games with your children

How does playing games relate to learning responsibility? Games are a great way to teach kids about rules, and much of responsibility is about following rules. In addition to demonstrating that there are right and wrong ways to take actions to produce desired results, games also teach about winning and losing. Rather than allow the kids to throw a tantrum and pout when they lose, use the opportunity to teach some life lessons.

They can learn that when one person wins, others inevitably lose, and this is true throughout life. They learn that losing is not always bad, as long as it's done gracefully, and that even winning should be done with class. Part of responsibility is learning to overcome the failures, and keep moving forward.

They may even learn that if they keep working on a skill they're not particularly good at, they *will* improve and eventually become a winner themselves. It's the old "try, try again" maxim, but it's true.

> *Rules are a major part of living;*
> *fun should be a major part of learning them.*
> ~ John Harmon Chapin

How I've accomplished this:

Know when to bend the rules

"Rules are rules" and *"Rules are meant to be broken"* are two opposite ends of the spectrum. If rules you've made are going to be broken, they should only be broken by you, and only be broken because you realize that life is not black and white, and that "stuff happens."

If you've instituted a strict curfew, and Jenni has always honored it, but just this once she wants to stay out an hour later for a concert, there's no harm in allowing a later curfew for a special occasion. Of course, you will have checked the concert times, and know who she will be with. Let her know that it's only because she has been responsible with past curfews that you're allowing this exception.

By being willing to negotiate this scenario, you will avoid the argument that surely will follow, and you'll let her know you aren't completely heartless. But most importantly, you're giving her an opportunity to prove her responsibility. If she lets you down this time you won't negotiate next time. And by giving her this chance, you will have won her cooperation with future rules and curfews.

*Remember – it's not about **winning**, it's about raising responsible kids!*

How I've accomplished this:

Help them learn from mistakes

When a young child breaks a dish or loses his lunchbox, and your reaction is to yell at him and tell him how clumsy he is, he'll be afraid to come to you when he makes the big mistakes! You will already have made it clear that slip-ups are not acceptable in your household.

Errors and accidents are not the exclusive domain of the young. As adults, we've all had our share. So we can't—nor shouldn't—expect that our children will never make a mistake while growing up.

When they do err in some way, help them (without criticizing) to find the lesson in it. Then drop it and don't bring it up again. They'll respect you, and feel safe telling you about their future—possibly life-changing—errors in judgment.

Keep lines of communication open, and your child will use them.

How I've accomplished this:

Don't allow excuses or blame

Responsibility means owning your actions. If you allow them to play the blame game or make excuses for their bad behavior, they'll continue the practice well into adulthood. At that point, they'll be talking to people who don't love them the way you do; people like bosses, clients, customers or cops. These people won't be nearly as understanding as you were.

Teach them that the best words in a tough situation are often "I'm sorry. I made a mistake." To reinforce that those words are the right ones to use, you need to make sure your reaction reinforces that message. If you explode when they 'fess up, they'll hesitate to do so again.

Listen calmly, praise them for taking responsibility for their actions, help them learn from the mistake, discipline them if necessary (if it was a willful act, rather than a mistake), and move on.

> *"You can't change what you don't acknowledge."*
> ~ Dr. Phil McGraw

How I've accomplished this:

Help them learn to use their money wisely

Allow your children to handle their own money, but teach them to do so responsibly. An allowance—besides giving the kids some extra spending money—can provide the perfect opportunity to teach financial responsibility. There is much debate about whether allowance should be tied to chores. One point of view is that it's best not to "pay" Ben for individual jobs done, but rather to help him realize that rights and responsibilities are tied together. Allowance is a right, and chores are a responsibility. If he doesn't accept the responsibilities, he may lose his rights.

For children old enough to understand, use the analogy of driving—if he doesn't drive safely, (responsibly) he may lose his license (right).

Instead of just providing money to spend on his wants—consider giving him enough to also buy lunches, pay club dues, purchase birthday gifts, give to charity, and to save. Depending on his age, you might want to monitor his spending/saving for a while, to make sure he's got the hang of it. After a while, with any luck, his budget will become habit.

> *"A fool and his money are soon parted."*
> *Teach your child financial wisdom, not foolishness.*

How I've accomplished this:

Don't micro-manage

Children won't always do things the way we would. That's okay; they're still learning. To mangle an old saying *"Anything worth doing, is worth doing imperfectly."* Allow them to do some things their way—and don't go back and fix it!

If you asked Jake to make his bed, and it looks like his entire G.I. Joe platoon is hiding under the blankets, don't worry about it. Praise his efforts. He's more likely to improve with praise than with constant criticism and "fixing" on your part.

If Lana wants to wear the orange shirt with the purple pants and red socks, tell her she looks very colorful and let it go. If you insist that everything be "matchy-matchy," she may give up trying to dress herself, and have trouble making decisions later in life.

When you accept your child's decisions and choices, even if they're not perfect, you provide them with a sense of accomplishment and responsibility.

There are plenty of critical areas where you *will* want to have the last word. Let them make some decisions on their own, and don't worry about the ones that aren't hurting anyone.

Allow imperfection, so they can enjoy a sense of accomplishment.

How I've accomplished this:

Make expectations clear

Setting expectations early on will alleviate any misunderstandings as children get older. If you expect them to do their homework immediately after coming home from school, stick to that schedule until they realize it's a normal routine. Otherwise, you'll continually be nagging at them to do their homework; after school, after dinner, before bedtime, on weekends, etc. They won't have any solid expectations, and so will continually put it off until they "feel like it." Meanwhile, you've turned into a nagging machine, and they're not learning to take their responsibilities seriously.

Expectations can extend into areas such as which chores they're responsible for, how they treat others, how much money they will save from allowance, and how clean their room should be kept.

Don't confuse expectations with rules, though they often accomplish the same thing. Expectations should become habit, while a rule is usually for a specific act or situation, and would probably have punishment for infractions.

Today's expectations become tomorrow's responsibilities

How I've accomplished this:

SELF ESTEEM

There is overwhelming evidence that the higher the level of self-esteem, the more likely one will be to treat others with respect, kindness, and generosity.   ~ Nathaniel Branden

Building self-esteem is a sticky issue. Of course we want our child to feel good about herself and develop confidence. But some studies show that if we tell our child she's the smartest person in class, even when her grades show otherwise, we're actually doing more harm than good.

Teachers who give out undeserved "A"s may be developing a strong—but false—sense of self-esteem in their students. Those kids who graduate from high school without having really *earned* the grades or diploma will find a tough time ahead when completing college entrance exams or going on job interviews.

As the adults responsible for raising confident and responsible kids, we should do what we can to build self-esteem, but do it in a way that does not offer false beliefs in their talents and abilities. When telling your child something positive, ask yourself "Is this true or possible?" If it's not, look for something else encouraging to say that is either true now, or possible with work on their part.

In everything you say, be sure that it's uplifting, not destructive. Dr. Phil McGraw says *"It takes a thousand 'attaboy's' to erase one 'you're not good enough, you idiot'."* *Never* make your child think he or she is not good enough. Children crave their parents' approval—often well into adulthood. Let them know from the beginning that you love them unconditionally, and demonstrate your approval through your words and actions.

Be supportive of his dreams

If Joel has his heart set on trying out for Pop Warner football, you'll do him no favors if you remind him that he's the smallest boy in his class, or he can't even catch the balls you toss him in the yard. Allow him to at least try, give as much encouragement as you can, and he may surprise you by being the fastest runner on the team. But if he continually misses plays, don't tell him he's the best player the team ever had. He may believe you, and stop trying to improve.

We can't always support everything our kids want to try, but by encouraging them in activities that could help them realize a talent or skill, we help them learn what they can do well. When they know their strengths (and weaknesses) they can feel better about themselves, and dare to step out and take risks when tackling the bigger things in life: SATs, college exams, or job interviews.

"Children are likely to live up to what you believe of them."
~ Lady Bird Johnson

How I've accomplished this:

Help kids believe in themselves

Similar to the previous tip, but this one goes a step further. Being supportive means *don't discourage* your children from their dreams.

Helping them believe in themselves means to *actively encourage* them when they struggle with self-esteem issues.

When one of Courtney's ventures or projects isn't going well, and she's ready to give up, encourage her to hang in there and look at it from other angles. Point out some other options she might try, and reiterate the skill or talent that will help her move forward. Suggest books or other helpful materials that might provide further insight into the problem.

Remind her that many things in life require hard work and tenacity, and that giving up won't help her achieve her goals.

> *Believe in your dreams and they may come true;*
> *believe in yourself and they **will** come true.*

How I've accomplished this:

Point out strengths and skills

Whenever you see your child do something especially well, be sure to point out that they seem to have a particular aptitude for it. We're not talking about how well they make their bed, or set the table, but areas where skill or talent is involved. If Kyle is carving a model ship, and doing a really good job, compliment his precision and steadiness of hand.

When Alison sketches a skillful design for redecorating her room, emphasize that she may have a flair for art or design.

Their interests may come and go, but perhaps the skills that were involved are indicators of future hobbies or careers. Kyle may end up being a surgeon and Alison could become an architect!

> *If you hear a voice within you say 'you cannot paint,'*
> *then by all means paint, and that voice will be silenced.*
> ~ Vincent Van Gogh

How I've accomplished this:

Help overcome or face a weakness

Humans are not equally blessed with talent, skill, strengths and weaknesses. Our kids need to realize that there are just some things they may not do as well as their siblings or friends do.

If Patty loves playing piano, but just can't get the hang of playing smoothly and confidently, help her try different tactics. Perhaps she could change her practice times so she's more alert. Maybe a different teacher could bring out the best in her playing. Or it could be she'd play better if she were playing music she likes, rather than what she's forced to play. Any of these options might help her overcome a perceived weakness.

Or … you may all need to face the fact that she just really doesn't have a talent for piano. If everyone agrees that's the case, allow her to relax and just play for her own entertainment. If she's not worried about being perfect, she'll enjoy it more. Eventually she'll find another interest in which she excels.

"Once we know our weaknesses they cease to do us any harm."
~ Author unknown

How I've accomplished this:

Start an 'Attaboy/girl' list

Often, our kids don't see the value in what they have achieved. They tend to think they can't do anything well. If your child feels like this, have him sit and write down everything he can think of that he's done well. Offer suggestions when he bogs down. The accomplishments don't have to be lofty—after all … he's a kid!

Call this the "attaboy" or "attagirl" list, and encourage them to add to it as they experience more successes.

Even younger children can list things such as: learned how to tie his shoe, won the class spelling bee, got an "A" on the poem he wrote, had his drawing published in the school newsletter, came in first in the footrace in the park, or picked some flowers for the sick little girl in the neighborhood.

A teen can write that she passed her driving test on the first try, read fifteen books during the summer break, was elected class president, ran in a 5K, or helped repair a house for a deserving family.

Be sure to include volunteer activities, so they can understand that giving to others is as important as getting recognition for their own accomplishments.

It's important that they realize this exercise is to help *them* feel good about themselves, not to show why *you* love them. Make sure they understand that you love them for themselves, not their accomplishments.

Nothing builds self-esteem and self-confidence like accomplishment.
~ Thomas Carlyle

How I've accomplished this:

Make a 'feel-good' list

This is a good exercise for anyone—especially a child who may be going through that "I can't do anything right!" or "I'm a dummy" phase.

It's different from the "attagirl/boy" list in that the former list chronicles past *accomplishments*, while this one is to create an inventory of current *traits*, *talents*, and *skills*.

If Linda is feeling down in the dumps, sit down with her and have her make a list of all the good things about herself. This list should focus more on personal or character traits, rather than accomplishments. If she's having trouble coming up with items for her list, feel free to jump in and remind her of things you like about her. Include traits such as her kindness, compassion, neatness, willingness to help, her big smile, the pictures she draws for you, that she does her chores without complaining, etc.

Make a game of it, and make sure she comes up with a list of at least 20 items. Be sure that she contributes most of the items, so she'll realize some of her own best features. Keep the list and have her look at it, and even add to it regularly, especially when she gets into the doldrums again.

> *Trust yourself … you know more than you think you do.*
> ~ Author unknown

How I've accomplished this:

Save the mementos

When Laurie gets her name in the school newsletter, or even a real newspaper, cut it out and display it on the refrigerator for a while. Then put it in a scrapbook or an "attagirl" file for her. Not only will it be physical evidence of your pride in her, but it'll be something she'll look back on and enjoy years later.

A friend's son brought home the school newsletter in which a poem he had written had been published. His dad glanced at it, said "That's nice, Ray," and laid it aside. Later Ray found it in the trash can, and ran sobbing to his room. He felt that what he had done—and was so proud of—was meaningless and worthless in his father's eyes. When the dad realized how he'd hurt Ray, he felt bad, and managed to reassure him. But how much better it would have been if Dad had spent a few minutes to acknowledge Ray's creativity and his initiative in writing the poem and submitting it for publication.

These kinds of recognition, even if only honorable mentions, can also provide fodder for the child's list of accomplishments discussed in a previous tip.

What we remember from childhood we remember forever -
permanent ghosts, stamped, inked, imprinted, eternally seen.
~ Cynthia Ozick

How I've accomplished this:

Celebrate!

When Justin graduates from kindergarten, wins the class spelling bee, or gets his Eagle Scout badge, make a celebration of it!

Our family usually went out for dinner, or sometimes just dessert in honor of an occasion. But an ice cream cone or a favorite treat at home could be just as special.

Whatever you decide to do, make sure it's known that it's in the particular child's honor. And if one child seems to excel more than the others, look for ways to celebrate the achievements of all, so their siblings don't feel left out. Celebrate when they write their name correctly the first time or read a picture book out loud by themselves.

Even though you're celebrating achievements, be sure you also express your pride and love for *who they are*, not just what they do.

Celebrate your own successes as well: Mom got a promotion, Dad was elected club president, or—working together as a family —you *all* finally got the garage clean. Treat yourselves to something special.

Any reason to celebrate makes for a fun and happy family.

How I've accomplished this:

Teach good communication skills

Encourage Jesse to reply to adults with more than one word, and to look others in the eye when speaking to them. But *don't* embarrass him by prompting him what to say during an attempt at conversation. If your neighbor asks Jesse, *"How's school going?"* and Jesse says, *"Fine,"* you should let it go for the time being. Later, talk to Jesse and demonstrate how he might have added something like *"I'm good at math, but history is hard for me."*

You might use a rubber ball to demonstrate that just as it's no fun to play when you throw a ball to someone and they keep it, it's no fun to ask a question and not get a full reply. They should toss the ball back (offer more information) to make conversation interesting. And who knows ... the neighbor might just have some tips on how to remember history dates!

If you teach a child these conversational skills while he's young, he won't be afraid to ask a teacher why he got a low grade, and he'll be less likely to get flustered when he goes for his first job interview.

Communication skills build confidence!

How I've accomplished this:

Encourage good health habits

A healthy body is a major contributor to a healthy self-esteem. The teen who goes to school in dirty clothes, with unwashed hair and fuzzy teeth is not likely to have many friends. Begin early to instill good hygiene rituals, so that they become automatic as he grows up.

Kids are going to eat whatever they can get away with, and we often have little control over what they eat when not in our presence—especially teenagers. But we can at least make sure they understand the basic concepts of nutrition and well-balanced meals. Explain how good eating habits will actually help them be more alert in school, as well as be stronger and more fit for the sports and other activities they want to pursue.

Keeping healthy snacks—rather than chips and sodas—available at home, and preparing well-balanced meals will help instill the importance of healthy eating.

When we feel good physically, we feel better emotionally.

How I've accomplished this:

Encourage problem-solving

It's often tempting for us to jump in and solve all the problems our child is facing, rather than let him work them out for himself. But if we do this too often, he won't learn the problem-solving skills that are so crucial later in life.

Rather than offer an immediate solution, allow him some time to think about every angle of a situation. Encourage him to write down pros and cons if it's a tough decision he has to make. You might offer suggestions on ways to approach the problem, without offering to solve it for him.

If he can come up with an answer himself, he'll feel good about his ability to solve the problem alone. And it'll give him the confidence to tackle more difficult challenges as they arise.

The parents' greatest job is to prepare their kids to be adults.

How I've accomplished this:

Encourage journaling

Journaling is a great way to work through feelings and concerns. Just getting issues down on paper helps to solidify all the murky thoughts that often seem to flit around with no purpose, and yet weigh heavy on our hearts.

Girls tend to like the idea of journaling more than boys. It's easier for them to pour their emotions out onto paper. Some boys think journaling is "sissy," so you may have to change the vocabulary or tactics.

In either case, if they don't want to keep an on-going journal, at least provide them with a notebook or let them choose a journal they like, and suggest they write out concerns, and then list ways they might be able to overcome the problem.

Remind them they can also use the journal/notebook to record good things that happened to them, accomplishments, and future goals. It's the perfect place to record the "attaboys" and "feel-good" lists mentioned earlier.

If they don't see it as an *assignment* to write something in it each day, they'll be more likely to turn to their journal when they need to work out problematic issues. And if they record the positive things that happen on a regular basis, they'll have the added benefit of realizing that the good times generally outweigh the bad. When they recognize how much good is done to and for them, and how much they do for others, they'll feel better about themselves overall.

Writing down our accomplishments reinforces our self-esteem.

How I've accomplished this:

TIME

Don't count every hour in the day,
make every hour in the day count ... for your kids.

It seems that today everyone is strapped for time. Often both parents are working outside the home. Clubs, organizations and civic activities take up our after-work time, plus the never-ending household chores. Even the kids have their own activities that keep them on the go.

Finding time to spend together can be difficult, but it's so important, that it needs to become a higher priority than dusting, club meetings, or social events. The time we spend with our kids while they're young is an investment that will pay huge dividends when they're older.

Even teenagers won't mind spending time with us if we make it a pleasant occasion, not a time to criticize them for their shortcomings or nag them about unfinished chores. Our children enjoyed doing things with us all through their teens, and still do as adults.

Don't confuse "quality" time with having to entertain them. Often, all your child needs is just an opportunity to talk, take a walk with you, or to tell you about their day. Nor should quality time be restricted to a certain period or number of hours each week. It should be an on-going process, as often as you can manage it.

Spending time together will benefit you as much as your child. While they're getting the benefit of your love, care, support, and teachings, you will have wonderful memories to look back on once they're grown. And you'll have no regrets of having missed their childhood because you were too busy to be there.

Read to your children

When you read to a child, you're letting her know that—during those minutes—spending time with her is exactly what you want to be doing; that you'd rather be with her than anywhere else. Reading to your children is a great way to spend quality time with them. It's calming for them, and relaxing for everyone. Little children love to be read to, and enjoy cuddling up to Mom or Dad during the reading. Something is being shared, forming a bond that grows stronger with every story time.

The Children's Reading Foundation says, "Just 20 minutes a day reading aloud with young children strengthens relationships, encourages listening and language skills, promotes attention and curiosity, and establishes a strong reading foundation."

When a child gets too old to be read to, you might ask her to read to you. As she gets older, you can discuss the books or articles being read, and may even be able to address some issues that have come up in real life.

The most important thing is the time being spent—time for just the two of you to share.

Read to your child today and create a lifetime of memories.
~ The Children's Reading Foundation

How I've accomplished this:

Plan activities they enjoy

Instead of always just dragging the kids along to events you enjoy, plan some activities you know they will like. Take your little leaguer to a real baseball game, or your ballerina-in-training to see the Nutcracker.

Plan picnics in the park, boating, kite flying, or visiting the fire or police museum. Go to carnivals, fairs, and the circus.

You could surprise them with a special event you know they'll enjoy, or let them help plan a day out.

Either way, when you make plans, you might also mention that you appreciate how well they've done with their chores, or in school, or even just how nice they've been lately. Whether you intend it or not, they may make the connection that good behavior equals good times!

We can't put "time in a bottle," so enjoy time together while you can.

How I've accomplished this:

Show up at events

Just being there for a child means much more than empty words ever could. Showing up for school functions, games or recitals demonstrates to Mike that he is more important to you than your work or other activities. All children want their parents to be proud of them. But it's difficult to demonstrate that pride if you're not there to see them hit the home run or play a solo in the concert.

Of course, sometimes work commitments, illness or emergencies prevent us from being there even when we'd really like to. When you absolutely cannot attend an event, be sure to set aside some one-on-one time afterward so your child can tell you all about it. Then express your pride, and perhaps offer a small celebration … ice cream sundaes, or a special day you'll spend with them.

Just be sure that the words, *"I had to work late"* or *"I had a meeting,"* don't become the standard excuse for your not showing up at events. The child will become cynical about your reasons, and may quit asking you to attend.

> *As important as the words "I love you" are,*
> *your presence is love in action.*

How I've accomplished this:

Focus your attention on one

Try to set aside at least an hour a week with each child, where it's just the two of you. Choose an age-appropriate activity, such as seeing a movie, playing a game, eating out, reading to them, going for a walk, shopping, or just sitting and talking. But try to ensure that nothing will interrupt that time: No cell phones, TV, business, or checking email should interfere.

The time doesn't have to be spent having deep heart-to-heart talks, but it should be something you both enjoy doing.

If you have three or more children, it may be difficult to set aside an hour per child one-on-one. Get the other parent or caregivers (grandparents, etc.) involved in sharing the one-on-one time. If you think you just don't have time, consider what's really important; getting the laundry folded right now, or letting your child know he's the most important thing in the world to you.

This hour does *not* mean that you don't have to be involved the rest of the week. Spend as much time as you can with all the kids, as often as you can. Just try to have some one-on-one time at least once a week.

The time you spend now, will pay off later,
when you want your grown kids to spend time with you!

How I've accomplished this:

Go for walks together and talk

For some reason, lots of good talks come out of just walking together. Maybe because it's a non-threatening atmosphere, maybe because you're not looking directly at each other, or maybe just because walking is a pleasant experience.

Start a routine of walking with each child for a short time once or twice a week, just for the fun of being out together. (This can be the one-on-one time in the previous tip.)

It's especially helpful—if you sense something is bothering your young one—to invite her to go for a walk with you. She may balk, but tempt her with a treat upon your return, or a stop for ice-cream along the way.

Use the time to ask non-probing, open-ended questions to try to draw her out. Even if she doesn't talk about problems, you may end up discussing other issues, or you might just have a pleasant walk together. Either way, it's good exercise, and time well spent.

> *"We have two ears and one mouth so that we can listen twice as much as we speak."* ~ Epictetus

How I've accomplished this:

Take them to lunch

I've probably told my kids more about my life over a meal, than under any other kinds of circumstances.

There's something about food that makes every experience more fun and interesting. Sometimes just going to lunch— whether it's a fast-food place with your preschooler, or a nice restaurant with your teenager—can add an element of closeness and sharing. It's more than just doing things together, such as shopping and errands; it's a time to sit, relax and talk. And somehow, lunch is more casual and relaxing than dinner. But any mealtime is a good time to learn more about each other.

This can also be one of your one-on-one dates, or you could take all your kids at once. Just make it clear that there will be no boisterousness, that this is a special time to talk and find out about each others' current happenings.

If your child's school allows, it can sometimes be fun to surprise him by picking him up for a lunch date, and returning him to school. It provides a nice break from his daily routine, some time together, and sends him back feeling a little bit special.

> *When sharing a meal together,*
> *it's easier to share our thoughts and feelings.*

How I've accomplished this:

Take your child to work

There is an actual "Take your Daughters and Sons to Work Day," which falls on the fourth Thursday in April. Several organizations sponsor similar programs, and age ranges vary, so check with your employer about their participation and requirements.

If your company participates in the program, or is just willing to let you bring your child along, then do so. If your son or daughter is old enough to understand and appreciate seeing what you do for a living, they'll enjoy spending the day watching you at work. It will de-mystify a lot of what you talk about when you're home.

Explain your job, and how what you do contributes to the company's mission, and ultimately, to society, whether it be a dry-cleaning establishment, or a micro-chip manufacturer.

This is a good time to explain how the right career can bring great satisfaction, and that a good education is key to doing what you love in life. Help your child think about what their career goals might be.

*Discussing career opportunities early on can capture
a child's imagination and help him set goals for his future!*

How I've accomplished this:

Include your kids in your activities

When our children were young we occasionally brought them along to our Toastmaster meeting, where good communication skills are taught and practiced. They were sometimes invited to participate in the meeting, by telling a joke or answering a Table Topic question. As a result, though neither of them have joined a club themselves, they are both confident speakers who are comfortable talking in front of groups, with hardly an "um" anywhere in their conversations!

Explain to your child the purpose of any service club or professional organization you belong to, its goals, and how your membership contributes to others or benefits you.

If you're on a sports team, be sure to have the kids attend your games. Even if they don't play sports themselves, they can learn about fair play and sportsmanship by watching you compete.

Taking them with you not only gives them an opportunity to see what you do, but it also provides a chance for you to spend time with them before and after the event, answering their questions or discussing what they learned from the experience.

Experience—not lecture—provides the best education

How I've accomplished this:

Make meal time a positive occasion

The daily family dinnertime ritual is almost a thing of the past. If all of your family still sit down to dinner at the same time, you're already off to a great start! To make it even better, try to ensure that it's a happy, positive experience. Discourage any bickering, negativity, complaining or whining. Ask about funny things that happened during the day, or have each person share one success.

Even if your family is scattered in 14 different directions with activities, try to schedule one or two "firm" dinner times each week. Maybe Tuesday is the only night that everyone has free, and Sundays are usually a casual day at home. Establish a schedule of family dinners on those two days—and instill a sense of responsibility in the family members to be there. Make those two mealtimes as important as anything else on the schedule, and let nothing short of an emergency interfere.

Then keep it a happy, uplifting experience, and the family will begin to look forward to that time together.

The dinner table is about more than just dinner.
It's about sharing conversation, manners, and thoughtfulness.

How I've accomplished this:

Plan an occasional "date day"

I once bought tickets for my teenage son and myself to see Bob Newhart perform on stage. We were both big fans. That evening, we went to dinner and the show, and called it our date. So that my daughter (who didn't *"get"* Newhart) wouldn't feel left out, my husband planned a date with her. He bought her flowers and took her out to dinner at a very nice restaurant. Each child loved their "date-night."

When my husband and son made a big to-do over watching the Super Bowl together, my daughter and I would spend the day out. We'd go shopping, to lunch, and a movie or two. Everybody was happy!

If you can plan several special days a year with each child, they'll look forward to it during the in-between times. Alternate between Mom and Dad, so each child gets time with each parent. Take them to breakfast, shopping, lunch, a movie, or any of a hundred other activities. To make it really special, let them choose what they'd like to do for part of the day, and you plan the rest.

The age of the child will determine whether you spend an hour or an entire day. A five-year-old may be tired after an hour or so, while a twelve-year-old can go all day long if you let him.

It's not how much activity you can fit into a day...
it's how much love!

How I've accomplished this:

Let them work with you on a project

Kids love helping their parents on projects, whether it's preparing a meal, planting a garden, or building a doghouse. Sometimes the "help" is anything but. Nevertheless, it's a great opportunity to teach your children skills, work together, and spend time with them. While working together, you can discuss many things other than the project itself. Even having your son tear up the lettuce for the salad gives you an opportunity to discuss anything from his day to healthy eating!

By letting a child work on bigger projects with you, you're demonstrating your confidence in him and allowing him to try new challenges, which in turn will build his confidence.

The next time you're planning a garage sale, let the kids help clean, organize and price items. When you have to do a 500-piece mail-out for your club, let Emmy stuff envelopes with you. If you're assembling a toy or a piece of furniture, let Dennis hand you the parts he can identify, as you need them.

It might take you a little longer than doing it yourself, but the extra benefit of building a relationship will make it worth every minute!

The fastest *way to complete a job is not always the* best *way.*

How I've accomplished this:

VALUES

We do not act rightly because we have virtue or excellence,
but we rather have those because we have acted rightly.
~ Aristotle

The term "values" means different things to different people. It can mean anything from accuracy to fairness, to perseverance, to wisdom, and much more. Basically, our values are *our* opinions of what is important to *us;* what we consider to be a valuable trait.

The values I'm going to discuss are obviously ones I think are most important, especially as they pertain to raising confident and responsible children. These are the values I'd most like to see in an adult. You may think of other values you deem to be more important. And that's fine. Make a list of what traits you'd like to see your child acquire, and then check parenting websites, books, or magazines, to find ways to instill those in your child.

You'll notice I have two tips on Trust, because I think it's critical that trust works both ways in a relationship. In fact, to be effective, it can *only* work both ways.

Trusting You

When you make a promise to your child, do everything in your power to keep it. If you tell Greg you'll be at his game, don't let anything get in the way. If you told Andrea she could have the new bike for her birthday, don't change your mind later on.

Of course, sometimes the unavoidable happens. If you're on your way to Greg's game when your car breaks down, and you can't make it in time, call if you can, to let him know. When it's absolutely impossible to keep a promise, make sure they understand that it was unavoidable—that it wasn't your choice—and that you didn't just blow them off or forget.

When they trust you to keep your word, they'll be more likely to keep their word to you. When they do let you down, you can use the examples of how you kept your promises to them, to make them understand how you feel when they disappointed you. Ask them how they would have felt, had you not shown up at the game, or not come through with the bike.

Trust is a two-way street.
Since you're the grown-up, you have to set the example!

How I've accomplished this:

Trusting Them

We told our kids, *"We'll always trust you until you give us a reason not to."* It had quite an impact, since they didn't want to lose the trust they already had, and so they did their best not to let us down—and rarely did.

Long after they were grown, our daughter told us that—while in high school—her big brother insisted they leave a party when they discovered alcohol was involved. What really touched our hearts was that he knew that if there was trouble, it would reflect badly on us—especially their dad, who was Chief of Police at the time. They loved and respected him enough to not want to cause him pain or problems.

It's important that you let your children know you trust them to do the right thing. But it's also vital that they *earn* that trust. By giving them small responsibilities, and seeing that they carry those out as they should, you can teach them how trust and responsibility go together.

However, once they've broken that trust—by coming in after curfew or lying—you need to impress upon them that they will now have to rebuild the trust, and that it will take time. You might set a time period—a week, a month or a year—depending on the seriousness of the violation. Once they've proven themselves over that period, you can give them trust they deserve.

Trust has to be earned, and should come only after the passage of time.
~ Arthur Ashe

How I've accomplished this:

Tolerance

There's no place in this world for prejudice, discrimination, or even teasing those who are different from ourselves. Whether the difference is ethnic, religious, physical or mental, everyone deserves respect from everyone else.

In addition to personal differences, tolerance also refers to accepting weaknesses, failures, or inadequacies in others that we may not have. If the waitress keeps forgetting to refresh your water, or neglected to bring part of the order, rather than express anger or sarcasm, accept that she may be having a bad day, might be ill, may have problems on her mind, or perhaps she's just not as efficient as others. Tolerance means acceptance—in all kinds of situations.

Set these standards for your children while they're very young, and if you discover them acting in a way that hurts others, take steps immediately to make sure they understand your expectations.

> *When children learn acceptance early,*
> *they will become caring, compassionate adults.*

How I've accomplished this:

Appreciation

It seems many of today's youth have everything they could possibly want, yet still find more "stuff" they absolutely must have. If this applies to your kids, they may need some lessons in understanding the value of their possessions, as well as the cost.

When they're made responsible for paying all or part of the cost of a new item, by either saving for it, or working to earn it, they'll have a better appreciation for what it takes to get and maintain the things they want in life. When they realize that it takes them ten hours of mowing the lawn, for example, to earn the new computer game they can't live without, they'll better understand the time, effort and money involved in acquiring the big ticket items such as cars, when they reach that point.

In addition to their possessions, teach them to appreciate the little things in life: the random acts of kindness, the thoughtfulness of others, spending time with friends and family, and what they already have.

If you can't appreciate what you already have,
more won't make you happier.

How I've accomplished this:

Faith

Children who have a solid foundation of faith feel more connected to the world and to others. They don't feel quite so alone when the chips are down. Whether the rituals, guidelines and teachings of an organized religion, or just belief in a higher power, faith provides a grounding effect that can pull a child through some tough times and carry on into adulthood.

Spend time talking to your children about your spiritual beliefs. If you don't have any, you might want to research different faiths, to see if there's something there that appeals to you as a family. It has been said that *"The family that prays together, stays together."* Whether you believe that or not, it is true that having a common belief gives a family a place to go spiritually when times get rough.

Without faith nothing is possible, with it nothing is impossible.
~ Mary Mcleod Bethune

How I've accomplished this:

Environmental responsibility

No matter what your thoughts or beliefs about the state of the environment, there are certain actions that are just common sense, and morally responsible.

Instruct your children not to throw trash anywhere but into a trash receptacle, and clarify what items should go into the recycle bin. Help with a "Clean Up the Park" day, or take other opportunities to help clean or restore public areas.

Teach them to not be wasteful with our resources. Remind them to turn the water off while brushing their teeth, turn lights and appliances off when leaving the room, and to not leave doors to the outside open when heaters or air-conditioners are running.

Not only will these simple tips help the environment, but they'll make things a bit easier on your budget as well!

A good incentive to encourage using less power is to make note of your current electric bill, then be very conservative with power usage the following month. Compare the next bill to the first, and if it's significantly lower, give a portion of the savings to each child. They'll be learning environmental and fiscal responsibility, as well as building habits that will take them into adulthood.

For other ideas on how to get kids involved in the environment, go to www.epa.gov/kids/

The environment they save today will be theirs tomorrow!

How I've accomplished this:

Cultural awareness

In order to have a good set of values of all kinds, your children should be exposed to some of the finer things in life, such as art, good music, museums, and even good restaurants.

If you only take your child to fast food restaurants or coffee shops while they're growing up, they may feel intimidated when walking into a nice restaurant with white tablecloths. Let them experience this early on, as soon as they're old enough to behave without disturbing other diners.

Our children not only were comfortable in nicer restaurants, but they had confidence when ordering their own meals or asking questions of the waitstaff.

Helping them to value cultural environments will give them the knowledge and insight to dismiss those things that are not as worthy; rock music with vulgar lyrics, drugs, or the myriad of other negative influences that are out there to tempt our youth.

Don't force your values or interests on your children, and don't try to mold them into a little you. It's important to let them be themselves. But do consider exposing them to the arts and museums as part of their education, so they'll discover who that self is.

Expose your kids to the best influences,
so they'll more easily recognize the worst.

How I've accomplished this:

Success

It is said that a picture is worth a thousand words. In any event, some kids understand and relate better to visual stimulation more than all the verbal encouragement we can give. If Joel's goal is to become an astronaut, find a great poster of the moon landing, and hang it on the wall. Next to it, put the steps needed to achieve that goal; good grades, college degree, discipline, physical fitness, etc.

Jen might prefer having a scrapbook of architectural drawings, or buildings that she likes, to inspire her toward her goal of becoming an architect. Again, have her include the steps required to achieve that goal, so that she can stay on target.

By having an objective and the necessary actions in front of them on a daily basis, the kids can stay focused, and will probably make better decisions; basing those decisions on how they will affect the ultimate goal.

Holding a goal constantly in front of you nearly ensures its success.

How I've accomplished this:

Fairness

A favorite shout of most children (especially teenagers) is, *"It's not fair!"* Sometimes, instead of trying to explain why something *is* fair, it's best to just agree and say, *"You're right, life is not fair for anyone, and you're no different."*

You might point out people she knows to whom life has been very unfair; the school friend who is a paraplegic because of a car accident, or the family who lost their home because of extended illness or unemployment. Then help your daughter to realize that not getting the expensive new jeans she had her heart set on is a relatively minor disappointment.

Maybe Winter lost a competition she felt she should have won, or Skyler wasn't chosen for the football team.

It's disappointing, for sure; but don't let them dwell on it. Help them to accept defeat and disappointment gracefully, and to move on to their next challenge.

> *Life is not fair, and is often difficult.*
> *Accept the former and overcome the latter.*

How I've accomplished this:

Excellence

Children are usually looking for the easy way out. It's their nature. In their preschool years, all they have to do is play. As they get into school, they have new responsibilities, but play is still their highest priority when deciding how to spend time. So they may cut corners with their chores, or rush through their homework, doing a slipshod job of it.

When you discover this, take the opportunity to teach them the benefits of working harder—and more carefully—for greater satisfaction.

You might explain to Mike that if he took more time and care building his model car, it would look better and last longer. Or if Ricky did the job right when mowing the lawn—instead of rushing over it haphazardly—it might not need to be mowed quite as often.

Self-help author and speaker Brian Tracy says, *"The foundation of a lasting self-confidence and self-esteem is excellence; mastery of your work."* By learning to do some tasks well, your child will build the confidence to try more difficult challenges in the future.

Remind him that the easy way is not always the best way, and it sometimes results in more work in the long run.

> *We are what we repeatedly do.*
> *Excellence, then, is not an act, but a habit."*
> ~ Aristotle

How I've accomplished this:

Morals

You don't want to micro-manage everything your child does, but you do want to keep tabs on what they're exposed to on a daily basis. It's a good idea to monitor what they read, watch, and listen to. Do some research on their favorite bands, skim through the books or magazines they read, watch TV or DVDs with them.

If you find that they're into something you don't approve of, rather than over react—sit down and calmly discuss why you don't want them engaged in that particular brand of entertainment. Let them know the negative effects these kinds of influences can have. You'll probably get some *"everybody else does it"* arguments, but stand firm.

Of course they may still listen to unacceptable music, experiment with drugs, or become involved in sexual activity when they're away from home. You can't watch them every minute. But if you give them calm, rational explanations, they'll be less likely to get in over their head, and they'll at least know you don't approve of what they're doing.

If you start educating them early as to what is right and good, and what is negative, harmful and destructive, they'll be more likely to listen to the years of training, rather than the peer influence of the moment.

"Bonding with parents is the cornerstone of moral development."
~ Dr. Ian Russ

How I've accomplished this:

126

Work

We all love to give what we can to our children, and it's fine to do so ... to a point. But if they are always given everything they want in life, they'll never learn the value of work, or the joy of earning what they get.

My five-year-old grandson had saved $70 of the $80 needed for a particular Lego set he wanted. He saved gift money, did extra chores, and even created a series of finger paintings to sell to his adoring grandparents and aunts. When he visited us recently, I made sure he was able to "earn" the last $10 needed (after all, I'm the Grandma.) But the point is, he spent five months earning and saving. The $80 toy was not just handed to him because he wanted it. He'll appreciate it much more, having waited so long and worked for it. (As a side benefit, he learned a bit about becoming an entrepreneur!)

Help your child figure out how he can either earn the money for what he wants, or perhaps give up something else he's spending money on, whether it be comic books or CDs, to save toward his goal.

Giving our children everything they want—even if we can afford it—gives the false impression that the material things in life come easy if they just whine, nag, or harass long enough. We want our kids to learn that they can still get what they want—if *they* are willing to work to make it happen, rather than rely on others to provide it for them.

Some people dream of success...
while others wake up and work hard at it.
~ Author Unknown

How I've accomplished this:

Acknowledgements

My first writing group, the Wild Women Writers, was instrumental in helping me fine-tune the ideas during the early days of this book. Later, my good friends, also writers and editors, Lana Swearingen and Laurie Hosken, provided exemplary editing help.

John Chapin, who read the draft, offered suggestions, and kept me on track to get it done.

Dr. Phil McGraw, who, though we've never met, has reassured me that much of living a responsible life is just common sense.

My husband, Fred, has always supported me in every endeavor, and after forty years of marriage, is still my biggest encourager. And I am his biggest fan!

And, most importantly, I must thank our two adult children, without whom I would have no basis for this book. My husband and I may have been good parents, but Joel and Jen were fantastic kids: a pleasure to raise, and now a joy to have as friends.

OTHER BOOKS BY DEE DEES:

LifeNotes Life-writing Kit - includes forms, photo pages, title pages, organizers and more. Makes a great gift! $ 49.95
> *(available April 1, 2013)*

Write Your Life Story in 28 Days **$18.00**
can be ordered online at www.lifestorylady.com
or by completing the order form and mailing to the address below.

Quantity	Item	Unit cost	Total
_____	LifeNotes Life-writing kit	@ $49.95	$_____
_____	Write Your Life Story in 28 Days	@ $18.00	$_____
_____	Raise Confident and Responsible Kids @ $15.00		$_____
	Arizona Residents add 7.3% sales tax		$_____
	Add $8.00 postage for each LifeWriting Kit		$_____
	Add $3.00 postage for each book		$_____
		TOTAL	$_____

Complete info below and mail with check or credit card info to:

LifeGuides Press   368 E. Gilbert Road   Gilbert, AZ 85295

Name:_____

Address _____

City_____ST_____ ZIP_____

Credit Card Type: Visa____ MC_____ Expiration Date:_____

Number: _____